Allen S. Weiss /

Varieties of Audio Mimesis:
Musical Evocations of Landscape

Allen S. Weiss

—

Varieties of Audio Mimesis: *Musical Evocations of Landscape*

Errant Bodies Press

… for the birds …

From dissemination, a transmission;
from transmission, an interference;
from interference, a complicity;
and from complicity, the sound of something dripping
in the darkest caverns of the cerebral cave.

Gregory Whitehead

I rejoice that there are owls. Let them do the idiotic and maniacal
hooting for men. It is a sound admirably suited to swamps and twilight
woods which no day illustrates, suggesting a vast and undeveloped
nature which men have not recognized. They represent the stark
twilight and unsatisfied thoughts which all have.

Henry David Thoreau

OVERTURE

—

In his journal entry for 18 November 1837, Henry David Thoreau notes: "Nature makes no noise. The howling storm, the rustling leaf, the pattering rain are no disturbance, there is an essential and unexplored harmony in them. Why is it that thought flows with so deep and sparkling a current when the sound of distant music strikes the ear?"[1] For Thoreau, to listen is already to think, to compose, and all natural sounds are musical, all music evokes a world. Furthermore, Orpheus, the god of music, is always in tune with his epoch, as Thoreau wrote on 23 January 1852:

No music from the telegraph harp on the causeway, where the wind is strong, but in the Cut this cold day I hear memorable strains. What must the birds and beasts think where it passes through the woods, who heard only the squeaking of the trees before! I should think that these strains would get into their music at last. Will not the mockingbird be heard one day inserting this strain in his medley? It intoxicates me. Orpheus is still alive. All poetry and mythology revive. The spirits of all bards sweep the strings. I hear the clearest silver, lyre-like tones, Tyrtœan tones. I think of Menander and the rest. It is the most glorious music I ever heard. All those bards revive and flourish again in that five minutes in the Deep Cut. The breeze came through an oak still wearing its dry leaves. The very fine clear tones seemed to come from the very core and pith of this telegraph-pole. I know not but it is my own chords that tremble so divinely. There are barytones and high sharp tones, etc. Some come sweepingly seemingly from further along the wire. The latent music of the earth had found here a vent. Music Æolian. There were two strings, in fact, one each side. I do not know but this will make me read the Greek poets. Thus, as ever, the finest uses of things are accidental. Mr. Morse did not invent this music.[2]

In this modern version of the classic trope of the wind through the trees —
roughly contemporaneous with Baudelaire's theory of correspondences —
Thoreau describes a form of audiophonic mimesis that is a prefiguration of
both synaesthetic poetics and synthesized music. It is precisely the difference between these two forms of audiophonic mimesis — the familiar simulations of the mockingbird and the bizarre novelty of the Aeolian telegraph
harp — that might well serve as an emblem of the study that follows.

Thoreau further claims, perhaps with some hyperbole, "the telegraph
harp has spoken to me more distinctly and effectually than any man ever
did."[3] Sarcastic and ironic as his claim might be, he probably didn't realize
how radical such an idea could be in terms of the history of musicology
(not to mention communication theory). For Thoreau's experience of the
"latent music of the earth" does not seem to be an instantiation of the
phenomenon that Leonard Bernstein evokes in his reflections on telluric
poetry: "I believe that from the Earth emerges a musical poetry, which is by
the nature of its sources tonal."[4] Rather, Thoreau's sundry observations on
the musicality of the environment bespeak an early modernist imperative
of training the ear to hear the discrete sonic transpositions in the natural
soundscape (the mockingbird's imitations of both natural and artificial
sounds, in turn mimicked by the poet's onomatopoeia), and of attending to
the radically novel innovations fostered by the incursions of technology into
the natural environment (the telegraph-harp, the steam locomotive). As we
shall see, these new sounds, as they progressively enter the musical domain,
are precisely what shattered the tonal harmony of both the celestial spheres
and the profound earth.

Over half a century later, in 1911, Ferruccio Busoni thematized the
essential role of sliding tones in nature, noting that they were effectively
suppressed by the very structure of the European musical system of equal
temperament. While he claims that, "all arts, resources and forms ever
aim at one end, namely, the imitation of nature and the interpretation of
human feelings," he nevertheless laments the fact that the division of the
keyboard instruments into twelve equidistant degrees has, "so thoroughly

schooled our ears that we are no longer capable of hearing anything else — incapable of hearing except through this impure medium. Yet Nature created an *infinite gradation — infinite!* Who still knows it nowadays?"[5] This infinitude, this trajectory of transcendence in music, is the vortex that shall guide the present study.

Perhaps the earliest modernist example of such ethereal music is Henry Cowell's short composition, *Aeolian Harp* (1923), played directly on the strings of a piano. He describes these glissando effects:

> *Natural sounds, such as the wind playing through trees or grasses, or whistling in the chimney, or the sound of the sea, or thunder, all make use of sliding tones. It is not impossible that such tones may be made the foundation of an art of composition by some composer who would reverse the programmatic concept, such as expounded by Richard Strauss. Instead of trying to imitate the sounds of nature by using musical scales, which are based on steady pitches hardly to be found in nature, such a composer would build perhaps abstract music out of sounds of the same category as natural sound.*[6]

The aim of *Varieties of Audio Mimesis* is to elucidate the relation between both mimetic *and* abstract sounds as they reveal the depths of the natural world and the lineaments of our own phantasms.

The history of European musicology is perennially revised around a central ontological debate: whether music is a representational or an abstract art. This discussion may be extended to all of the sound arts (of which music is a subset). *Varieties of Audio Mimesis* attempts to reveal the extent to which the mimetic function is not only present in music, but also essential to its interaction with the other arts. I would propose, as a set of working hypotheses: (a) the difference between abstraction and mimesis forms a fundamental aesthetic aporia; (b) there exists an implicit nexus of synaesthesia and heterogeneity in all arts, such that every art form has correspondences with, explicitly or implicitly, all other art forms; (c) every art form has as its ideal a *Gesamtkunstwerk*, an ideal art form englobing all the arts; (d) formal transpositions are possible between all art forms.

Ultimately, every epoch has a different paradigm of the total work of art: 16th century: opera; 17th century: gardens; 18th century: the encyclopedia; 19th century: Wagnerian opera and the novel; the first half of the 20th century: cinema; the second half of the 20th century: the various mixed-, multi-, and inter-media works; and today, at the beginning of the 21st century: virtual reality. (The present study, for the sake of a coherent periodicity, shall mainly restrict itself to the pre-digital analogue epoch.) Gardens, for example, constitute a primal *Gesamtkunstwerk*, the site of all sites, the ground of all the arts, the unstated nexus of heterogeneity in the system of fine arts, the source of synaesthesia, the analogue of all correspondences.[7] To consider landscape in this manner would be to remove the Hegelian curse upon the history of gardens: the placement of landscape architecture at the bottom of the aesthetic hierarchy, due to the fact that gardens constitute a material, hybrid, incomplete, mutable, alterable art form. Quite to the contrary, it is precisely this *hybridity* that permits the garden to operate as the fulcrum of the interchange between nature and culture, and to serve as the substratum of the relations between the sundry arts; and it is such *incompleteness*, based on growth and change (both formal and aleatory) in the landscape, that permits synaesthetic interchange between the senses. Every aspect of garden design offers itself to complex intertwinings and transmutations: parterres based on dance steps, millefleur tapestries and millefiori glass designs; topiary imitating sculptures and ornaments; paths organized according to architectural perspectives; illusions calculated by mathematical formulas; scale measured by military ballistics; the picturesque inspired by perspectival painting. Conversely, garden representations appear in all the arts, both the "minor" ones of fabric design, glass-blowing, pottery, pastry decoration, fireworks, etc., and, of course, the "major" ones of literature, poetry, painting, and music. Such transpositions between different arts constitutes a source of creativity which inevitably returns to haunt, or inspire, garden design. In relation to the art of gardens, the mimetic aspect of words and sounds, however obscure, however rarified, offers a particularly rich path of investigation. Such would be the foundation of a "unified field theory" of music and landscape, as the following analysis will attempt to show.

Thus each art form is not a unique, isolated aesthetic domain, but rather a nexus at which all other art forms are centered (or decentered, as the case may be), within a complex matrix of intertwining reciprocity and reversibility. These issues need be rethought today, at the moment when heterogeneity and synaesthesia have become paradigmatic concepts in aesthetic and epistemological discourse and museological practice. The study of audio mimesis (with onomatopoeia as a minor subcategory), necessarily demands that attention be given to the synaesthetic intertwining of soundscape and landscape, heretofore given little attention.

The question of mimesis is at the origin of Western aesthetics and linguistics, and it continues to inform our artistic production, theory and critique. The *locus classicus* is Plato's *Republic*, where ontology and epistemology are defined according to varied levels of representation: the intelligible world consists of pure forms, which are imperfectly represented by mathematical objects; the inferior world of appearances is constituted by visible things, in turn represented by images, themselves finally devolved into shadows. In this schema, mimesis is the art of imitation and transposition, whereby formal paradigms are recreated as sensible particulars. Needless to say, art — as the copy of a copy, the ultimate mimesis — is near the bottom of the ontological hierarchy, represented by the famed shadow theater in the cave of the *Republic*. But what if we were to invert the hierarchy, and deem the shadow theater of the Platonic cave — full of melancholy and mystery, more attuned to the imperfect and finite courses of our lives — to be of the essence?

In Plato's *Cratylus*, the theory of mimesis is discussed in relation to the nature of language. The title character, Cratylus, insist that there is a natural meaning to words, and that the sound of words somehow bear their sense (the naturalist theory), while his opponent, Hermogenes, argues that the meaning of words is a function of social processes (the conventionalist theory). Is the relation between word and thing natural or artificial? Is the relationship between sound and sense motivated or arbitrary? Though most post-Romantic linguistics has opted for the conventionalist model — a theory given great impetus by Ferdinand de Saussure's early modernist concept of the arbitrary relation between signifier and signified — there always existed some quotient of mimesis in even the most recalcitrantly anti-mimetic theories. The issue can be summed up in what is one of the central aporia of linguistics, regardless of the theory in question: language is, in ever-shifting degrees, expressive *and* referential, sensual *and* significative, mimetic *and* conventional.

Johann Gottfried von Herder claimed, in his influential *Treatise on the Origin of Language* (1770), that the *Ursprache*, the primal language, was a sensuous one of "sheer verbal luxury and joy," free from grammar and syntax.[8] To the contrary, as contemporary linguistics has shown, language is always linked to the world, however tenuously, however equivocally, through its mimetic faculties. Sound is sensual *and* meaningful, a structured articulation of body *and* world. The text of the world is noisy, not silent. It should be remembered that Socrates ultimately dismissed Cratylus' arguments, and sardonically suggested — in a sort of auto-allegorical moment within his own dialogue — that Cratylus take a walk in the countryside, escorted by Hermogenes. Yet it is of course here, in nature, that the mimetic faculty abounds, and the two philosophers strolling through the woods might well have heard the strains of a natural music that would one day inspire musicians, poets and philosophers of a different mold, such as Thoreau. And yet, the conclusion to this Socratic dialogue can itself be historically allegorized. It is said that at the end of his life, Cratylus was convinced by the Heraclitian notion of the eternal flux of all things, and in despair of attaining philosophical truth, gave up the use of language. In response to his disciples' queries, he would consequently — like so many Zen masters after him, like Wittgenstein at the limits of his own discourse — only point to things. Somewhere between Cratylus' silence and Herder's joyful cacophony lies the sonorous existence of landscape and the visual evocation of sound.

The famed Saussurian definition of the linguistic sign as being composed of the arbitrary relationship between signifier and signified entails that the signifier exists only as the difference that separates it from all other signifiers (acoustic images). According to this theory, the material aspect of language (sonic, phonic) is accidental, not essential, to meaning. However, several alternate linguistic theories, in great part inspired by the work of Roman Jakobson, argue for the meaningfulness of language at the phonetic level. According to this research, the differential feature of language is not determined by the differences *between* phonemes (as for Saussure) but by the differences of distinctive features *within* phonemes. First discussed by Nikolaj Trubetzkoy, the systematic classification of the phoneme seen as a bundle of differential sonic elements was theoretically established in 1938 by Jakobson. While there exists a quasi-universal set of phonological differences that subtend nearly all languages — vocal/ non-vocal; consonantal/non consonantal; compact/diffuse; grave/acute; nasal/non-nasal — this is not to suggest a univocal or universal symbolism of sounds, not even within a given language.[9] But it points to the fact that linguistic sounds have their own characteristics, organized and experienced in terms of those binary oppositions — sharp/dull; open/closed; rough/ smooth, etc — implying a certain level of prelexical onomatopoeic symbolism, and consequently a broader level of synaesthetic correspondences.[10] This emphasis on vocal formations also suggests the corporeal, even erotic, foundation of linguistic meaning. Whence the importance of the onomatopoeic function: onomatopoeia, while not being elevated to rank of the origin of language (as certain 19th century linguistic theories would have it), is far more than a special case, an accidental feature of language, as Jakobson explains.[11] For there indeed exists a primal sound-sense that underlies discourse.

Owing to the neuropsychological laws of synaesthesia, phonic oppositions can themselves evoke relations with musical, chromatic, olfactory, tactile,

etc. sensations. For example, the opposition between acute and grave pho-
nemes has the capacity to suggest an image of bright and dark, of pointed
and rounded, of thin and thick, of light and heavy, etc. This "sound sym-
bolism," as it was called by one of its original investigators, Edward Sa-
pir, this inner value of the distinctive features, although latent, is brought
to life as soon as it finds a correspondence in the meaning of a given word
and in our emotional or aesthetic attitude towards this word and even more
towards pairs of words with two opposite meanings.[12]

To put the issue most succinctly, as Claude Lévi-Strauss stresses, "the linguistic sign is arbitrary a priori, but ceases to be arbitrary a posteriori,"
when it is necessarily motivated.[13] This is humorously illustrated by the art
historian Ernst Gombrich, citing an experiment suggested by Jakobson:

It is my conviction that the problem of synaesthetic equivalences will cease
to look embarrassingly arbitrary and subjective if here, too, we fix our at-
tention not on likeness of elements but on structural relationships within a
scale or matrix.... I have tried out this suggestion in a party game. It con-
sists of creating the simplest imaginable medium in which relationships can
still be expressed, a language of two words only — let us call them "ping"
and "pong." If these were all we had and we had to name an elephant and
a cat, which would be ping and which pong? I think the answer is clear. Or
hot soup and ice cream. To me, at least, ice cream is ping and soup pong.
Or Rembrandt and Watteau? Surely in that case Rembrandt would be pong
and Watteau ping.[14]

Two broad areas of investigation suggested by such phonically motivated
synaesthesia are worthy of note: *epistemologically*, the problematic of the
erotics of speech, *i.e.*, the specific pleasures of vocal articulation, whether spoken or sung, conscious or unconscious; *metaphysically*, the fact that
the least common denominator of speech consists of meaningless binary
oppositions between distinctive vocal tendencies might well explain one of
the unconscious foundations of the binary or dualistic features of thought,

perhaps even more profoundly than the phenomenology of lived oppositions, such as up/down, left/right, empty/full. Consider a more concrete
example:

> *Each of the syllables* pif-paf-pouf *also constitutes a monosyllabic onomat-
> opoeia that serves to designate a unique sound; but they cannot be indiffer-
> ently used for any noise whatsoever…. The miners of Fontainebleau have
> three onomatopoeias to designate the diverse qualities of sandstone: they
> call* pif *that which is very resistant,* paf *stone of good quality, and* pouf
> *that which is reduced to sand at the slightest shock.*[15]

This structural matrix from which sense, meaning and image emerge is organized according to a gestaltist imperative, such that the least-common
sensory or linguistic denominator motivates an orientation in the world,
existentially situating the subject according to a primitive and provisional level of meaning. The specific meaning of *pif-paf-pouf* is a function of
the existential situation in which these vocables are enunciated; one can
well imagine a very different symbolic destiny for them as they are transferred to another anecdote or another situation.

Language is thus imbued with virtual images — or at least schemas that
give rise to images — at its very core. As part of his critique of Cratylus,
Socrates suggests what would appear to be a *reductio ad absurdum* of the
naturalist claim: if words have a natural meaning, so too do letters, such
that *rho* would express motion, while *delta* and *tau* express rest; *alpha*, size;
eta, length; *omicron*, roundness; etc. Despite such mockery, the mimetic
dimension of language is not as ridiculous as it sounds. Language is per-
meated with symbolism, operating on manifold ontological levels. For
example, one 19th century linguistic system suggests that primal symbolic
values adhere to all the letters of the alphabet: c = convexity and concavity,
e and j = involution and reflexion, i = verticality and unity, l = coming
and going, m = horizon and enclosure, o = rotundity, t = verticality and
horizontality, u = cavity, s = sinuosity, x = intersection.[16] To imply, as the
author does, that these correspondences are of univocal form and universal

applicability is to misunderstand the polysemic nature of language. But to grasp these correspondences in the manner of *pif-paf-pouf* — that is to say as symbolic markers in a limited system of signification, as exemplified by Rimbaud and the Symbolist poets — is to grasp a profound though arcane dimension of the richness of language.

In another, more metaphysical, system, "O symbolizes 'the infinite circle of time and space,' the universe, and more specifically the globe of the sun and by derivation its movement, heat and light. I, with its point that again represents the sun, is a line extended virtually to the limits of visibility, thus verticality, thus fire, thus anger; it is also the self (I) as the figure of a standing man, 'in his primitive state of innocence,'" etc.[17] Even more widespread among poets, artists and musicians is the claim of synaesthetic relations between vowels and colors, a correlation made famous by Rimbaud's poem *Voyelles* [Vowels] — A black, E white, I red, U green, O blue. This type of synaesthesia is shared (though always with differing sound/color correlations, and more generally with differing experiences of the nature and degree of the synaesthetic effects) by such figures as Hugo, Grimm, Scriabin, Nabokov, Messiaen, and many others. What was intended by Socrates as a sarcastic critique of Cratylus in fact generated a tradition with enormous ramifications — sometimes central, usually marginal, but always present in linguistics. The ultimate extrapolation of this theory is the belief in the universe as a hieroglyphic system, a cosmic book, which lead to investigations as diverse as the *hierobotany* that would study the language of flowers, the *hiero-astronomy* that would interpret the language of the stars, and the arcane domain of musicology devoted to the harmony of the celestial spheres.[18] Or, to put it in more contemporary semiological terms, all objects are fundamentally signs, and the world is a sort of rebus where sign, object and sound combine and recombine in an interminable and indeterminate process demanding perpetual reinscription and reinterpretation. Though these mimological assumptions may not be as foundational for linguistics as some have argued, they are also not quite as ridiculous as others have made them out to be — the grain of truth they contain is crucial for all linguistics, poetics and musicology. The sound-sense of words, like their image-sense, thus plays an integral role in the connotative generation of meaning.[19]

Among the first modernist instances of artistic experimentation concerning the inner structure of words is that of the Russian Futurist Velimir Khlebnikov, whose poetic *Zaum* creations based on "the interior declension of words" directly influenced Roman Jakobson's earliest linguistic studies, and eventually inspired the theory of the phoneme as a bundle of differential structures.[20] Three major implications of these always marginal and often eccentric or even mad mimetic theories obtain: (a) sound and sense are indissociable; (b) the relation between signifier and signified is not arbitrary but motivated (Roman Jakobson); (c) there is an interdependence between linguistic form and content (Louis Hjelmslev). Thus onomatopoeia and imitative expression are not merely rare special cases, but rather an integral (if partial) aspect of all language.[21] The dimension of meaning founded on the objective structure of phonemes is, as Gérard Genette (following Jakobson) suggests, simultaneously stable and universal *and* unstable and subjective: the relationship between signifier and signified is partially motivated, and the general form of this motivation is onomatopoeia. The major axes of Genette's monumental study on the subject, *Mimologiques*, are enumerated and summarized in his concluding chapter: "By qualifying the mimologist theory as 'fantasmatic,' I do not intend to designate a 'falseness' that is totally relative and not at all of our concern, but simply to connote the essential role played in mimological thinking, characterized by *wishful thinking*, by a complex and more or less conscious system of desires, let us say of predilections to be satisfied."[22] The list of linguistic characteristics leading to such idiosyncracies follows: substantialism (refusal of abstraction); preference for the most concrete elements of language, such as semantemes rather than morphemes, nouns rather than verbs, proper names rather than common names; the need for valorization (refusal of neutrality) that establishes preferences, such as that of one language to another, vowels to consonants or consonants to vowels, masculine to feminine, etc; the instinct of motivation (refusal of gratuitousness, horror of the semantic void); the taste for analogy (refusal of difference). The mimological function is thus a tendency, a means of determining a certain use-value of language, a realignment of sense in relation to its poetic possibilities. What Genette terms the "fantastic rectitude" of the sound-sense of words is just that: a means of generating reverie, fantasy, imagination, and even alternate worlds, from the most minute linguistic elements.

The subject is vast, fascinating, suggestive. The arts are all infinitely malleable, and each art form is permeable to all others, such that the hermeneutic key to all the arts entails the contradictory exigencies of *mimesis, transposition, metaphor, correspondence* and *rupture, montage, metamorphosis, disintegration*. However, these formal polarities can only make sense through consideration of the processes of *enunciation, transmission, broadcast*. To narrow these sweeping prefatory considerations down to the concerns of the present essay, we should especially note that representational systems must in all cases be investigated according to their microstructure, for the term "representation" *simpliciter* is so vast as to be practically meaningless. It is hoped that this study of the microstructures of audiophonic representation will serve as a sort of listening guide to reveal previously unheard dimensions of familiar music and to suggest unimagined forms of a future sound art.

ONTOLOGY

—

"I hear bees humming near the brook, which reminded me of the tele-graph harp," writes Thoreau in his journal entry of 22 April 1852.[23] What is curious here is the choice of onomatopoeia, for colloquially, we now usu-ally say that bees *buzz* rather than *hum*. (Here lexicography and etymology are helpful in a curious manner. The *Oxford English Dictionary* teaches that *buzzing* is a "sibilant humming," while a *hum* is a "low, continuous murmur-ing sound," and in turn a *murmur* is a "subdued continuous or continual-ly repeated sound." The subtle continuity between these definitions, and their potential circularity, suggest the profound complexity of such audio-phonic mimesis, all the while revealing possible modes and structures of transpositions and substitutions between sounds. We should never forget the degree to which lexicography and rhetoric are at the service of poetry.) Did Thoreau's choice of terms obtain because the genius of the language that has since transformed the hum into a buzz had already begun to dif-ferentiate the bee sound from that of so many machines that ceaselessly fill the soundscape with their drone? Or might this variance be caused by the more subtle need to create a correspondence between bee and Aeolian harp, thus choosing an onomatopoeia that sounds midway between the two? Or had Thoreau perhaps wished to capture the specific mix of bee and brook, which necessitated the attenuation of the hymenopterous com-motion by means of aquatic dampening? Compare the entry for 31 August 1852: "Landed near the bee tree. A bumblebee on a cow-wheat blossom sounded like the engine's whistle far over the woods; then like an aeolian harp."[24] One should note the correspondence between three radically dif-ferent sound sources, and (despite received opinion) his pleasure in arti-ficial sounds. This suggests that the mimetic quality of onomatopoeia is often not the simple, univocal (in the literal sense of the term: single vo-calization) phenomenon it is most often made out to be, but rather a het-erogeneous event of mimetic complexity, including spatial and temporal resonances as well as referential diversity. Auditory mimesis may range from a single reference to a complex tale. Thoreau extends the limits of onomatopoeia to the very core of language: "Hear the first brown thrasher, — two of them... They drown all the rest. He says *cherruwit, cherruwit; go ahead, go ahead; give it to him, give it to him*; etc., etc., etc."[25] In fact, he goes so far as to utilize onomastics (proper names): "Do I not hear the veery's *yorick*?"[26] Unlike the parrot, who simulates words, the veery approximates them, suggesting correspondences in the mind of the hearer, in this case a Shakespearean allusion. The thrashers' triple onomatopoeia (sounds, words, names) operates at all linguistic levels: phonemic, syllabic, lexical, even syntactic — in each case emotional quality is added (gain in connotation), while communicative signification is diminished (loss of denotation).

It is hardly surprising that in the chapter devoted to the five senses in Catherine Laroze's *Une histoire sensuelle des jardins* [A Sensual History of Gardens], the section on hearing is introduced by a paragraph teeming with onomatopoeia, nor that the major part of the text is devoted to the sounds of water and birdsong: "Songs that recount fleeting instants. An infinitude of sounds bursting forth to our ears: cracklings, chirpings, breakings, whistlings, rustlings... hummings, crumplings, snappings [*craquements, piaillements, brisures, sifflements, crissements, bourdonnements, froissements, claquements.*]"[27] The "history of the senses" continually fluctuates between the immediacy of sounds (with their linguistic representations as onomatopoeia) and the complexity of artistic creations (with a concomitant conceptual and spiritual awareness). This is made evident, for example, in Alphonse Karr's appreciation of the sonorous existence of water, cited by Laroze: "'Flowing water is simultaneously painting and music that causes sweet thoughts, charming reveries, and melancholic memories to flow from my brain like a limpid, murmuring stream.' Aquatic sonority penetrates the brain to liberate the most fluid, the most elusive, the most fluctuating ideas."[28] However clichéd, such pronouncements are revelatory: a detailed analysis of landscape sonority will determine both a profoundly poetic dimension of the ontology of gardens and a complex synaesthetic imperative at the core of language. The restricted neo-classical model of mimesis is infinitely complicated by the Romantic inmixing of the arts and the intermingling of the senses, culminating in the almost mystical instance when subject and object are confounded in a fusion of attributes and a confusion of meanings.

In *L'eau et les rêves* [Water and Dreams] Gaston Bachelard offers a definition that may well guide us in this study: "Liquidity is... the very desire of language. Language wants to flow. It flows naturally."[29] On the surface, this metaphor offers little more poetry or philosophy than the perennial "time and the river flowing." Yet the specifics of his analysis intimate the infinite correspondences between sounds and images, revealing the linguistic paradoxes and poetic complexities of our expressions of the natural world. These are correspondences in the Baudelairian sense of the term: "The most singular equivocations, the most inexplicable transpositions of ideas take place. Sounds have a color, colors have a music. Musical notes are numbers..."[30] For the *genius loci* is always a *genius locutionis*. To consider the resonances between the sonorous potencies of nature and our transformations of these effects in poetry is to investigate the grounds of the rarely studied role of sound in gardens, and to provide the aesthetic foundations for the history of the art of garden sound installations. From ancient times, innumerable devices were created to imitate natural sounds, such as water-powered bird chimes, pneumatic birds, serpents, lions, and so forth, on through such contemporary manifestations as Erik Samakh's sound installations such as the "electric frogs" in Alexandre Chematoff's bamboo garden in the Parc de la Villette in Paris (1990), simple chirping sounds that arise from the bamboo stands as one passes by.[31] Such imitations do not merely surprise and deceive, eliciting emotions cherished by the baroque sensibility; they also establish new focal points in gardens, transmuting perspectives, transforming attention, and transmogrifying phantasms evoked by the natural setting. With the advent of each new sound technology, the ratio between the senses changes, and all the arts are radically, though subtly, transformed.

Consider one onomatopoeic example dear to Bachelard, the verse from Goethe's *Faust* pronounced by the water nymphs: *Wir säuseln, wir rieseln / Wir flüsten dir zu.* [We murmur, we ripple / We warble for you; Nous murmurons, nous ruisselons /Nous gazouillons pour toi.][32] The very basis of signification is a function of transposition and transmission, offering, through sheer sonority, the promise of deliquescent pleasure. Here, a primal adequacy between onomatopoeia and mythopoeia, between language and landscape, sets the stage of the material imagination, with its balanced reciprocity between *contemplated nature* (*natura naturata,* passive principle) and *contemplative nature* (*natura naturans,* active principle), between *reproductive imagination* and *creative imagination.* One might ask why the adequate expression of the sound of a brook would require three or more onomatopoeia. In fact, anybody who has ever listened to the *murmur* of a brook or stream well knows that the indeterminate and incalculable irregularities of its course create a most complex soundscape, requiring a great repertory of onomatopoeia, such that the term *murmur* barely suffices. Different onomatopoeia referring to the same sounds are therefore not really synonyms, but differentiating vocables. Compare, for example, the list derived from Charles Nodier's *Dictionnaire raisonné des onomatopées françaises,* which includes the aquatic terms *bouillon, cascade, cataracte, murmure, rincer, ruisseau.*[33] One may easily test such sonorous assumptions visually. For example, as I write I am looking at a painting done by Simon Carr in September 1991 depicting the brook that passes through his family's property in the Berkshire region of New York. It is obvious that the different parts of the brook — as it *streams* over boulder, *strikes* against branch, *splashes* upon banks (note both the assonance and consonance) — create and evoke different sounds. While the sound of water running from a faucet might well be represented by a single onomatopoeia (though, as in all cases, the choice is vast, even if only because of the harmonic complexity and rhythmic irregularity of different drips), the adequate representation of the sounds of a brook necessitates a combination of terms.

Such correspondences are hardly limited to literature. Steven Feld, in *Sound and Sentiment*, his extraordinary study of the Kaluli people of Papua New Guinea, provides a detailed musicological analysis of the structure and symbolism of their song in relation to birds and water:

> *It seemed that water and waterfall terms were systematically employed as metaphors for sound structure: "Your waterfall ledge is too long before the water drops," "There is not enough flow after the fall," "The water stays in the pool too long," "There is much splashing"; these were typical responses Kaluli made to my melodies, which had unbalanced contours, abruptly ending phrases, overly centered lines, and poorly placed meter...*[34]

This symbolic system is not vaguely metaphoric, but specific to the structure of the music, where the notion of a tonal center is crucial, necessary to establish an ontological stability within the fragile and fluctuating environment of the tribe. In fact, the music both centers the symbolic system and orients the tribe within its environment, giving sense to the apparent chaos of the world:

> Sa *can stand alone to mean "waterfall," can prefix terms for parts or kinds of waterfalls, and can prefix verbs of soundmaking and textual organization. As it generically stands for "waterfall" in its usual context, it generically stands for the interval of the descending minor third in sound terminology. This is in many ways the most basic and most important interval for the Kaluli. It is found in the calls of the fruitdoves and stands alone as a symbol of sadness, isolation, and loss [....]* Sa-gu *is the onomatopoeic and generic term for "waterfall sound"; in musical terminology it means descent to the tonal center. When the tonal center is held for a long duration in song, it is called* sa-gulu. Gulu *is onomatopoeic for long continual flow at a waterfall. As a verb,* sa-gu-lab *means to sing a line that moves to and ends on the tonal center.*[35]

Sa is thus the fulcrum of the transpositions between language, music and world. We might at this point remember Gaston Bachelard's claim that, "the imagination is a sound effects technician [*bruiteur*], who must amplify or subdue. Once the imagination masters dynamic correspondences, the images *truly speak.*"[36] Truly speak, or in some cultures, truly sing.

This extreme complexity of the auditory imagination borders on chaos: structured by puns and barbarisms, lapses and agrammatisms, metaphors and analogies, the role of onomatopoeia is not merely that of imitation: even more profoundly, onomatopoeia effects a rupture in signification leading to renewed attention to the sounds themselves. Opposed to syllogism and logic, the poetic use of puns and onomatopoeia, adored by Thoreau, has become a commonplace since Joyce, who taught us to hear the vast multiplicity of our inner voices (many of which are not human) and to see the plurality of our inner worlds (most of which obey laws, physical and moral, quite other than those of our common universe). Voice interprets nature; nature enriches the verb. Inspired by Maurice Merleau-Ponty's analysis of "the prose of the world" and our capacity for "singing the world," Steven Connor elaborates the psychology of this process:

> *Children develop very early on a pleasure in vocally reproducing the sounds of the world — the creaking of doors, the wailing of sirens, the pattering of rain. This is more than onomatopoeia, which is to say, more than mere imitation. When one vocalizes a sound, one gives it to one's own voice, in order to give it its own voice. What is imitated in onomatopoeic voicing is the world's own capacity to give voice, in an enactment of the possibility that things in the world might be capable of and characterized by speech, and that the sounds of the world might be being uttered by it. I do not merely borrow, or capture this speech in reproducing the noises of the world; I seem to give the world the same kind of interior self-relation as is possessed by all entities that have a voice, a self-relation founded on the capacity of voice to shape a being in the air. I give the world an animate life by taking it as a voice; but the voice is not merely the sign of this animation, it is the very means by which animation is accomplished.*[37]

Despite his limited view of onomatopoeia as "mere imitation," Connor is well attuned to the representational dynamics of voice.

Contemporary linguistics has resuscitated the role of mimesis in the constitution of meaning, an attitude perhaps best summed up by Paul Valéry's claim, so important for Roman Jakobson's poetics, that a poem is, "that prolonged hesitation between sound and sense."[38] This is *a fortiori* the case for representations of water, the poetic effects of which exist simultaneously on the level of the phoneme, the word, and the sentence. Consider the effects of liquid consonants, implying a primal connection between the vowel *a* and the hydraulic imagination (*aqua, apa, wasser, water*) within aquatic onomatopoeia. As the French know so well, and as the French language epitomizes, the *genius loci*, while being the spirit of a place, also establishes the essence of cuisine. This genius is inscribed in language. Consider the restaurant *Michel Bras*, situated near the town of Laguiole, in the Aubrac region of France's Massif Central. Michel Bras' signature dish is the *Gargouillou*, the name of the most basic recipe of the region, *gargouillou*, a simple ragout of potatoes in *bouillon* (an onomatopoeia for boiling water). Bras raises this regional recipe to the level of haute cuisine, as his gargouillou consists of as many as three dozen vegetables, herbs, flowers and grains chosen from nearly a hundred possibilities that constitute this virtual recipe; each ingredient necessitates a separate preparation, and all are mixed and moistened in a light butter sauce emulsified with vegetable broth flavored with ham essence, then decorated with herbs, crystallized leaves, edible wildflowers, wild mushrooms, and pearls of parsley oil.[39] The name *gargouillou* is derived from the verb *gargouiller*: gurgling, bubbling, rumbling. It is variously an onomatopoeia for the sounds of the bountiful streams that run through the Aubrac, for the quotidian cooking process of this most simple dish, and for the borborygmi (another onomatopoeia) by which our bodies announce hunger. It thus reveals both the *goût de terroir* (the gustatory specificity of the region) and the archetypal relations between the natural and cultural differences of water: the cold water of a running brook and the boiling water of the kitchen pot, the zero-degree of cuisine.

But as cuisine necessarily leads to geography, land leads to language. Bachelard would trouble this rather stable, regional relationship by adding a mythic dimension that, furthermore, increases the poetic and mimetic density of the onomatopoeic effect.

> *One would never finish searching for all the doublets of the phonetic im-agination of water if one listened to the spouts and squalls, if one studied together the cries and caricatures of the gargoyle* [gargouille]. *To spit out the storm like an insult, to vomit forth the guttural invectives of water, it was necessary to attach to gutters monstrous forms, all mouth, thick-lipped, horned, gaping. The gargoyle endlessly jests with the deluge. The gargoyle was a* sound *before being an image, or, at least, it was a sound that imme-diately found its image in stone.*[40]

Bachelard's considerations of onomatopoeia seek a correspondence between word and object that far surpasses the restricted linguistic sense of the term: "sound is only a part of mimologism," such that linguistic studies must be raised to the level of rhetoric and poetics.[41] The narrow sense of onomatopoeia gives way to its poetic suppleness, and such poetry opens the path to a true ontology of the material imagination. Furthermore, if "water is the most faithful 'mirror of the voice,'"[42] as Bachelard insists (borrowing the notion from Tristan Tzara, who practiced onomatopoeic poetry), this hardly implies a univocal relationship between human vocalizations and natural soundings. The adequacy of description is a function of the transformative powers of language, and the charms of onomatopoeia depend precisely upon the *differences* between the natural sounds and their poetic echoes.

In a different, more restricted sense, one might consider in this light those specific, codified words, of which several thousand have been classified, that indicate seasonal themes in Japanese haiku. The complexity of haiku is to a great extent dependent upon the manner in which such words connote an entire scene.[43] Similarly, all aspects of audio mimesis (seasonal connotations and otherwise) are a function of the intersecting exigencies of perceptual gestalt organization (which establishes the formal structural homologies that result in representation) and conceptual encoding (which contextualizes this representation in the larger cultural field): the forms and degrees of mimesis vary according to the symbolic systems in which they appear. A croaking sound that in one culture evokes the edge of a lotus pond on a sultry summer night under the last crescent of the moon might in another culture merely evoke a single frog, or even be heard as sheer noise, evoking nothing at all. This also holds for both nouns and common names. The linguistic amplifications of the sense of place explains why the singularity of names enhances the singularity of site, as Marcel Proust knew so well: "Names exalt the idea that I held of certain places on earth, by making them more particular, and consequently more real."[44] Name is a crystallization of place, which explains much of the profundity and many of the excesses of the spontaneous interpretations of popular etymologies, especially the belief that place names reflect specific topological characteristics. A famed example is that of the provençal Mont Ventoux, whose name derives from that of the celtic or ligurian god Ventur, Vinturi, Venturius or Vinturius, a god manifested by the brutal north wind, the mistral, that eternally blows at the mountain's peak and is reputed to drive people mad. It is at the peak of Mont Ventoux that the mistral blows the strongest in Provence, whence the identification between wind and mountain. The mistral, like all wind, is an active psychological and metaphysical principle. It is also a metaphor of poetic inspiration, as Gaston Bachelard explains:

> *The* poetic breath, *before being a metaphor, is a reality that one may find in the life of the poem if one wished to follow the lessons of the* material aerian imagination. *And if one paid more attention to poetic exhuberance, to all the forms of the pleasure of speaking, softly, rapidly, screaming, murmuring, psalmodizing... one would discover an incredible plurality of poetic breaths.*[45]

The poetics of the wind constitutes auditory mimesis simultaneously at its most intimate and its most transcendent level. But linguistic mimesis — whether as primal poetry or sophisticated rhetoric — offers diverse pleasures of the text. Consider such onomastic inventions as the playwright Valère Novarina's list of 1,111 imaginary birds with which he ends *Le discours aux animaux*: "la limnote, la fuge, l'hypille, le ventisque, le lure, le figile, le lépandre, la galoupe, l'ancret, le furiste, le narcile, l'aulique, la gymnestre, la louse, le drangle, le ginel, le sémelique, le lipode, l'hippiandre, le plaisant, la cadmée, la fuyau, la gruge, l'étran, le plaquin, le dramet, le vocifère, le lèpse, l'useau, la grenette, le galéate..."[46] Compare my English version, which begins: pimwhite, sandkill, partch, barnscrub, stiltback, goskit, persill, peeve, phyllist, corntail, perforant, titibit, queedle, jewet, phew, marshquiver, graywhip, corvee, rillard, preem, peterwil, cassenut, flusher, willowgyre, trillet, silverwisp, eidereye, wheeltail, ptyt, jeebill, wheatspit... Here we thrill at the power of naming, and at the rare adequacy between name and thing, such as animals whose very names function as onomatopoeia for the sounds they make: *owl* (the French *hibou* is even better), *crow, whippoorwill, cuckoo, chickadee...* Denotative suggestiveness proffers connotative richness. To say that such naming provokes *illusions* is not a critique, but precisely the point, the very core, of the poetic enterprise.

The ultimate extrapolation of this theory is that of Charles Nodier, for whom — since language itself is poetry, precisely due to its mimological factor — true poems may consist of *single words*, and the masterpiece of each language is the dictionary. Every word would thus have infinite semantic depth, and would constitute an entire imaginary world. (Structural homologies often exist between poetry and pathology: in this case, language that eliminates syntax and is reduced to a series of discrete words constitutes a form of aphasia.)[47] When conceived at the beginning of the 19th century, such a theory was deemed insane; today, after Dadaism, Lettrism, Sound Poetry, Concrete Poetry, it seems to describe a limit-case in both epistemological studies of the constitution of meaning and psychological investigations of the forms of fantasy. In relation to the

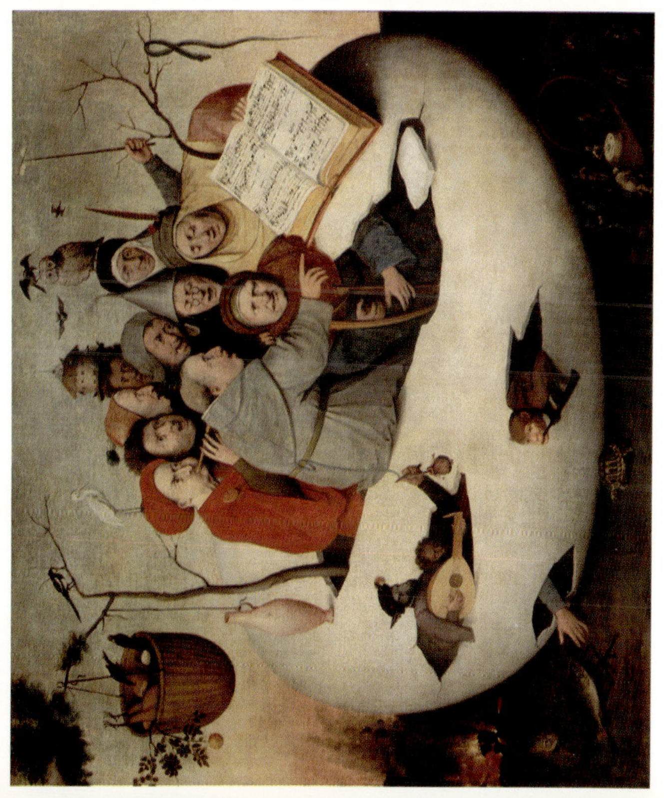

HIERONYMUS BOSCH – *The Concert in the Egg*, c. 1450 – 1516
(Palais des Beaux Arts, Lille, France)

expression of landscape, one may consider the work of Ian Hamilton Finlay — intertwining poetry and landscaping — perhaps best reflected in his *One Word Poem*:

Arcady

ABCDEFGHIJKLMNOPQRSTUVWXYZ

Like the chromatic scale in serial music, this poem contains all other poems. However, its site specificity — within Finlay's corpus, and more specifically in the context of his garden at Little Sparta — suggests something very different, unique, in relation to both the integration of poetry into landscape and the expression of landscape through poetry. The oldest philosophical tenet, Anaxagores' "Everything can be found in everything" — a theory repeated in Marsilio Ficino's neo-Platonic philosophy, Spinoza's pantheism, Swedenborg's mystical speculation, Baudelaire's correspondences, Hegel's dialectics, Borges' fantastic epistemologies — exists in its contemporary manifestation as the ontological and ecological belief in the universe as a holistic, unified system. Consequently, one can easily appreciate the following 19th century linguistic fantasy: "Justinus Kerner — physician, poet, theosophist — darkly identified the fiery gift of tongues, sleep-talking, the psycholinguistic effects of animal magnetism, and 'inner-language' — of which 'one word... frequently expressed more than whole lines of ordinary language, so that, after death, in one single symbol or character of it, man would read his whole life.'"[48] Doesn't this seemingly outrageous claim express all the mystery and power of the mantra, that magical incantation that condenses the essence of life into the endless repetition of a single sound, word or phrase? In any case, poetics must be founded on the ontology of breath, and the articulation of breath gives rise to rhythm. Speech is thus fundamentally lyrical, thus musical.

Bachelard's epistemology — where the real and the ideal exist in disturbing promiscuity — operates in diametrical opposition to the idealism of the neo-Platonic and Kantian traditions, as well as to the sensualism of Locke and Condillac. Inspired by Baudelaire's theory of correspondences —

where the ideal is compelled to excite all the senses — Bachelard celebrates ontological polyvalence and reversibility, entailing a sensorial metaphoricity irreducible to sheer sense data.

> *The sensations are hardly any longer the occasional causes of isolated images. The* real cause of the flux of images *is truly the* imagined cause *[....] the* function of the unreal *is the function that truly drives the psychism, while* the function of the real *is one of blockage, of inhibition, a function that* reduces *images in such a manner as to give them the simple value of a sign. It is clear that the immediate* contributions *of the imagination must be considered alongside the immediate* givens of sensation.[49]

Realism and classicism are subverted by an influx of Romantic idealism, where the quotidian and the contingent are interiorized as a system of symbols, and perception is produced autonomously by the psychic mechanism. Such correspondences attenuate the inhibitions imposed by the reality principle, establishing new ratios and relations between the senses. As Bachelard astutely remarks, "contradictions that would be intolerable in their initial sensible state come alive through a transposition into another sense."[50] This is hardly a Hegelian dialectical reconciliation of opposites, but rather the celebration of an aesthetics of inexactitude, an epistemology of perpetual poesis, slippage, transfer, metamorphosis, deviation.

Indeed, of all the elements, water is most favorable to such a sense of poetic decomposition and recombination, given its neutral qualities of osmosis that permit it to infiltrate everything and to be infused by everything, to reflect and refract, to be mobile and still, shallow and profound. Water is the element of transition and segué, of purification and catharsis. Meditating upon a passage from John Cowper Powys' novel *Wolf Solent* (1929), Bachelard notes:

> *The thrush, for example, sings like a cascade of pure water... the thrush's trill is a falling crystal, a dying cascade. The thrush does not sing for the sky. It sings for neighboring water... If nature's voices did not contain such*

> *onomatopoeic doublings, if falling water did not restore the accents of the singing thrush, it would seem that we could not hear natural voices poetically. Art needs to be instructed by reflections, and music needs to be instructed by echoes. It is by imitating that we invent.*[51]

These doublings, echoes and reflections (like those of Thoreau's bee and brook) not only denote the reverberation and resonance inherent in every sound, but also connote the referential correspondences within which each and every poetic image and sound are cast. This effect is well documented by Thoreau, in his journal entry for 22 April 1852: "The strain of the red-wing on the willow spray over the water to-night is liquid, bubbling, watery, almost like a tinkling fountain, in perfect harmony with the meadow. It oozes, trickles, tinkles, bubbles from his throat — *bob-y-lee-e-e*, and then its shrill, fine whistle."[52] The sophistication and precision of this multiple onomatopoeia attest to Thoreau's fine ear: the metaphoric and onomatopoeic "fountain" sounds of the birdsong (*bubbles, trickles, tinkles*), expressed in ornithological vocalese (*bob-y-lee-e-e*), are all finely nuanced by the site specificity of the meadow in which the red-wing was heard. One can be certain that if this bird had alighted in Thoreau's garden, the choice of onomatopoeia would have been subtly different: not because the red-wing would be harmonizing with a different landscape, (for it is ornithologically incorrect to suggest, as does Bachelard, that a bird sings *for* water, since birds sing only for birds), but because *we* would hear in its song a different harmony as the sounds and resonances of the garden replace those of the meadow. Thoreau's onomatopoeic metaphors are for us, not for the birds.

To hear water in a bird's song, to hear a bird's song in water, and to express these interrelations in poetry and music: the intertwining of nature and culture condenses in an inextricable nexus of sound and sense, music and phantasm.

FANTASY

—

The greatest poet of birdsong is Olivier Messiaen, many of whose melodies, and several of whose major works, consist of direct inscriptions or musical transmutations of the songs of birds: the third movement of *Quatuor pour la fin du temps*, entitled *Abîme des oiseaux* (1941), *Le Merle noir* (1952), *Réveil des oiseaux* (1953), *Oiseaux exotiques* (1955), *Catalogue d'oiseaux* (1956-58), *Chronochromie* (1960), *La Fauvette des jardins* (1970). It should be noted in this context that the first systematic sound recordings from nature were made by ornithologists. (Ironically, despite the ancient poetic resonances between birdsong and water sounds, the background sounds of running water are actually quite undesirable when recording birdsong.) In fact, the most imitated sounds in European music are those of water, wind, and especially birds, for after all, among all the animals, it is only birds who, colloquially stated, "sing." Messiaen's role as a recordist must not be underestimated. He collected and transcribed innumerable bird songs with the avidity of a true birder and the precision of a superbly trained musician and composer, believing that, "it is probable that, in the artistic hierarchy, birds are the greatest musicians that exist on our planet."[53] True virtuosi — there exist approximately 4,500 species, each with its own song — songbirds have extraordinary musical abilities. Though many birds have but a single song, the mockingbird has 250, the sedge wren about 400, and the brown thrasher over 2,000. But the situation is even more complicated, as recent research has shown that these songs are not merely inbred (genetically coded by species) but often also learned. In relation to their song, birds therefore need be considered not only as members of a given species (often singing in hybrid and regional dialects), but as individuals (with idiosyncratic styles and limitations). To stress the beauty of birdsong, Messiaen relates the anecdote of a professor of voice who bought an Indian shama, which, excited by the students' vocalizations, would sing throughout the lessons, imitating them so well and singing so beautifully that they often had to stop, ashamed of their own voices. (Incidentally, the first recorded birdsong, dating from 1889 in Germany, is that of a shama.)[54]

Messiaen's birdsong inspired works are indeed an instantiation of Bachelard's claim that, "It is by imitating that we invent." Messiaen created these works for standard musical instruments (rather than the electronic instruments then being developed), incapable of rendering the high pitches, micro-intervals (up to eighth tones), and the rapid elocution of much birdsong. Consequently, imitation led to stylization, restricted precisely by the limitations of standard orchestral instruments to the tempered scale, without recourse to extended techniques: the tessitura was dropped several octaves, melodies extended, tempos reduced, timbres transposed.[55] Messiaen only accepted certain of the lessons of the birds: rather than expanding the domain of tonality by the use of microtones or investigating new sources of timbre, his inspiration was mainly restricted to melodic and rhythmic invention. This nevertheless sufficed to bring musical mimesis to the fore.

The notation, imitation, and performance of birdsong is extremely complex. Thoreau queries: "What word can stand in place of a bird's note? You would have to bury it, or surround it with a *chevaux de frise* of accents, and exhaust the art of the musical composer besides with your different bars, to represent it, and finally get a bird to sing it, to perform it. It has so little relation to words."[56] Despite his protestations, Thoreau manages to do a better job than most inventing appropriate ornithological onomatopoeia. For another case in point, consider such transpositions from the marvelous *Dictionnaire des onomatopées*, where Pierre Enckell and Pierre Rézeau collect several variants on the song of that great natural musician, the nightingale (*rossignol*). The simplest is from Edmond Rostand's *Chantecler* (1910):

Tio ! Tio ! Tio !... Tio !

The most complex version — beginning with a variant of the simple *Tio !*

Tio ! Tio !... Tio ! — from Johann-Matthaüs Bechstein's *Histoire naturelle des oiseaux de chambre* (in its 1825 French "translation"), is quite another matter:[57]

Tioû, tioû, tioû, tioû,

Spe, tiou, squa,

Tiô, tiô, tiô, tio, tio, tio, tio, tix.

Coutio, coutio, coutio, coutio ;

Squô, squô, squô, squô,

Tzu, tzu, tzu, tzu, tzu, tzu, tzu, tzu, tzu, tzi.

Corror, tion, squa pipiqui.

Zozozozozozozozozozozozozo, zirrhading!

Tsissisi, tsissisisisisisisi,

Dzorre, dzorre, dzorre, dzorre, hi.

Tzatn, tzatn, tzatn, tzatn, tzatn, tzatn, tzatn, dzi.

Dlo, dlo, dlo, dlo, dlo, dlo, dlo, dlo, dlo

Quio tr rrrrrrr itz.

Lu lu lu lu, ly ly ly ly, liê, liê, liê liê

Quio didl li lulylie.

Ha gurr, gurr quipio!

Coui, coui coui coui, qui qui qui qui, gui gui gui gui.

Goll goll goll goll quia hadadoi.

Couigui, horr, ha diadia dill si !

Hezezezezezezezezezezezezezezeze couar ho dze hoi.

Quia quia quia quia quia quia quia quia, ti.

Ki ki ki, ïo ïo ïo, ioioioio ki.

Lu ly li le lai la leu lo, didl ïo quia.

Higaigaigaigaigaigaigai quiagaigaigai.

Couior dzio dzio pi.

While in *L'Abîme des oiseaux* Messiaen chose the clarinette, and in his first fully bird-inspired work, *Le Merle noir*, he preferred the flute — two "organic" wind instruments relatively close in timbre to birdsong — the majority of his subsequent ornithophilic pieces are for piano, not organic but rather the most mechanical of the classic instruments, more distant in timbre from birdsong but of greater rhythmic and dynamic virtuosity than most other instruments. By carefully imposing limits upon mimesis, Messiaen effectively *humanized* birdsong precisely by *stylizing* it.

Just as onomatopoeia evinces a reversibility between the verisimilitude of sensuous imitation and the expanses of poetic connotation, so too does Messiaen balance the two poles of mimesis (imitation and creation), combining the exigencies of music and science: "I used birdsong in two different manners, both in seeking to trace a musical portrait that is as precise as possible, and, to the contrary, by treating the birdsong as malleable material."[58] Nature and art, mimesis and stylization, are always permeable. For if he insists that his *Catalogue d'oiseaux* represents birdsong with an exactitude worthy of true bird-lovers, he goes on to explain that this verisimilitude extends to the regional specificities of the bird's habitat (as in Thoreau's onomatopoeia), including its ornithological neighbors and the varying manifestations of song during different times of night and day. For example, *Réveil des oiseaux* is organized according to the hours of the first half of the day (copying the monastic model — compline, prime, matins, sext — as the sense of the sacred is essential to Messiaen): *Minuit, Quatre Heures du matin, les Chants de la matinée, Midi*, and it includes the chants and cries of a nightingale, owl, skylark, blackbird, thrush and coocoo. While "respecting the solos, the great *tutti*, the small *tutti*, their places and proportions," all the birdsongs are accompanied in the harmonic and rhythmic dimension by the odors and colors of the birds' environment.[59] For Messiaen, ornithological denotation is always coincident with landscape connotation. These representational effects, though rare, exist in many forms, as may be witnessed in Junichiro Tanizaki's tale, *A Portrait of Shunkin*, where he writes of the musical prowess of trained nightingales in Japanese culture. The song of wild nightingales is restricted to such simple and rather unpleasant chants as *hokiibecha*. However, as the narrator explains,

> *But when you hear a bird as accomplished as Tenko, on the other hand,*
> *you are reminded of the tranquil charm of a secluded ravine — a rushing*
> *stream murmurs to you, clouds of cherry blossoms float up before your*
> *eyes. Blossoms and mist alike are within that song, and we forget that we*
> *are still in the dusty city. This is where art rivals nature. And here too is*
> *the secret of music.*[60]

(One wonders whether Bechstein's nightingale, given the astonishing rendition of its song, wasn't a trained one.) Mimetic connotation in both birdsong and music may thus attain the greatest complexity and refinement.

Messiaen, one of the composers most concerned with the relations between musical tone and visual color, effectively introduces a conception of synaesthesia at the heart of his mimetic operations. It is the entire natural context that is at stake in each work: the whole environment echoes in each bird's song, as transcribed and transposed for the human ear. The program notes for the *Catalogue d'oiseaux* are most suggestive in this regard, as they stress the natural, rather than the musical, context. Consider the text accompanying *Le Merle bleu — The Blue Rock Thrush (monticola solitarius)*:

> *The month of June. Roussillon, the Vermilion Coast. Near Banyuls: Cap*
> *l'Abeille, Cap Rederis. Cliffs overhanging the sea (Prussian-blue, sapphire-*
> *blue). Cries of Swifts; splashing water. The headlands stretch into the sea*
> *like crocodiles. Echoing in a rocky cleft, the Blue Rock Thrush sings. Its*
> *blue is in contrast to the sea: purple-blue, slate, satin, blue-black. Almost*
> *oriental, recalling the music of Bali, its song merges with the sound of the*
> *waves. Also heard is the Thekla Lark which flutters in the sky above the*
> *vines and wild rosemary. Herring Gulls scream far out to sea. The cliffs are*
> *awesome. Arriving at their feet, the water breathes its last — a memory of the*
> *Blue Rock Thrush ("like a choir of woman's voices in the distance...")*[61]

This fabulously hallucinatory, almost surreal, text illustrates what Bachelard saw to be the cosmogonic properties of onomatopoeia: stylized sounds

evoke an entire world, bathed in "onomatopoeic doublings" and synaesthetic delight. The scene evoked is not only a melange of the senses, but
also a veritable collage of sites, a confusion of color tones, a riot of mon-
taged birdsong, an ornithologization of the sounds of water, a surreal vi-
sion of the coast transformed into reptilian monsters, and ultimately the
anthropomorphization of birdsong and waves into the music of a distant
choir. (The hint of the Balinese should make one take note of Messiaen's
use of Indonesian modes and rhythms in his *Turangalîla-Symphonie* of
1948.) Moving well beyond the relatively commonplace synaesthetic relations between tone and color, Messiaen here suggests an ideal of total synaesthesia, an inmixing of the senses that not only enriches our perception
of the world, but furthermore creates a fantastic alternate world from the
rearranged and transmogrified elements of our everyday existence. Such
is music at its richest mimetic instance.

Bachelard's celebration of the "*correspondence* between the verb and the
real"[62] is inspired by the most cosmic expression of these ideas, Baudelaire's
sense of correspondences, where "everything in the Universe is an echo."[63]
In such a Spinozistic or Swedenborgian universe, where everything is
connected to everything else in an infinite set of correspondences, the
enjoyment and comprehension of any piece of music would necessitate
familiarity with all music. All music would be part of the music of the
spheres. But as man is not God, we must learn to listen, and each work
demands a spontaneous genealogy of the ear. The sonorous complexities
of the world may be represented by a vast musical synthesis, as in the
extraordinarily complex contrapuntal layering — so complex that it appears
to be on the verge of cacophony — of 18 different birdsongs, each with its
own rhythm and mode, in *Epôde,* part of Messiaen's *Chronochromie.* Yet it
is also the case, as in the *Catalogue d'oiseaux,* that a single onomatopoeia,
a single trill, might suffice to evoke an entire world.

TYPOLOGY

—

One of the major defenses of the imitative origins and functions of music is found in Charles Batteux, *Les Beaux-arts réduits à un même principe* [1746; The Fine Arts Reduced to a Single Principle], specifically relating the problem of musical mimesis to the visual arts:

> *There are two kinds of music. The one merely imitates unimpassioned sounds and noises and is equivalent to landscape painting. The other expresses animated sounds and relates to the feelings. This corresponds to portrait painting [....] A musical composition must be judged in the same way as a picture [....] What would we think of a painter who was content to throw on the canvas bold shapes and masses of the liveliest color without reference to any known object? The same argument can be applied to music [...] There is not a musical sound that does not have its model in nature.*[64]

Today, Batteux's position appears somewhat anachronistic, for indeed, the "bold shapes and masses of the liveliest color without reference to any known object," unthinkable as art in the 18th century, have become the very paradigm of modernist abstraction. Even more pertinently, non-emotionality and non-referentiality permeate the discourse of much modernist music, especially following the dodecaphonic revolution. Batteux clarifies the modes of mimesis (natural and human), and shows how the mimetic faculty applies to both impassioned *and* unimpassioned sounds, to both the human *and* the natural world. (Plato had already noted how certain musical modes touch the different passions and evoke more or less passionate responses than others.) The core of the musicological problem is summed up by the 18th century debate between Rousseau and Rameau, as musicologist Edward Lippman explains: "Rousseau saw music as akin to language, with its expressive force embodied in melody, which was an imitation of impassioned speech. Rameau viewed music as essentially

mathematical, with its foundation in harmony."[65] Subsequent musicology
has tended towards Rameau's abstract model, with the notable exception
of the field of ethnomusicology, a bastion of the mimetic theory. That said,
musicology and linguistics always reveal a mimetic function, whether conceived as a primal, essential foundation or marginalized as a merely occasional, accidental feature.

The allusion to landscape in Batteux is not incidental, as may be
extrapolated from the study of the hermeneutics of space. Postulating
imitation as the key principle of aesthetics, phenomenologically oriented
landscape theorist Philippe Nys focuses his discussion on the art of gardens,
"to the extent that this art is precisely at the core of the transposition not
only from nature to art, but also between the arts themselves."[66] These
operations of transposition constitute mimesis in the strict sense of the
term, but this should not be taken in a narrow manner, as Paul Ricoeur
stresses:

> *If we continue to translate* mimesis *by imitation, what must be understood
> is the contrary of the copy of a preexisting reality, and we must rather speak
> of creative imitation. And if we translate* mimesis *by representation, we
> must not understand by this word a redoubling of presence, as we can still
> hear in the Platonic* mimesis, *but the cut that opens the space of fiction.*[67]

It is such fictive supplements to landscape architecture — always apparent
within a synaesthetic matrix — that reveal the intricacies of the material
imagination, offering the garden as the very site upon which the arts are
scenarized. (Consider, for example, the great fête of 1668 at Versailles, including waterworks, fireworks, ballet, theater, music, fashion, cuisine.)[68]
One would do well to note the role of the only term used metaphorically in
the Ricoeur citation, the *cut* — the central trope of modernism in collage,
film, radio, music — space of the ellipsis, overture to the imagination.[69] The
richness of the imagination is in part a function of the ontological aporia
of sound art (and by extension of all representation): *mimesis is simultaneously a loss and a gain,* where the represented system (signified) loses

its structural integrity in the mimetic transposition, while the representational system (signifier) gains in phantasmatic complexity and epistemological ambiguity. Representation implies a fundamental incommensurability between terms, with consequent gains and losses. In the visual arts, for example, the classic distinction is the loss of tactile qualities through the two-dimensional representation of three-dimensional objects, with the concomitant gain of other qualities, such as the accentuation of structural relations and the addition of symbolic forms via perspectival organization. That said, the ontology and aesthetics of the sound arts, while being synaesthetically linked to the visual and textual arts, is radically incongruent with them. While the terms "representation" and "mimesis" are variously used across the arts, their form is in each case different. This suggests that musical forms cannot be fully assimilated to rhetorical figures.[70] These issues should not be lost on the sound arts.

*

The reflections on auditory mimesis that follow offer certain possibilities for grasping the ontological heterogeneity of contemporary music and audio art. The following schematization is offered not in order to establish rigid categories, but rather to give a sense of the vast multiplicity of mimetic functions in the sonic domain. For even the most cursory investigation of contemporary theories of audiophonic "representation" reveals the overly broad and impoverished use-value of the term.

Categorization of phenomena inflects ontology. In a sense, there are two broad types of categorization: either derived from family resemblances between objects, which are then sorted out according to a relatively limited number of differences; or derived from a limited number of distinct characteristics, according to which objects are subsequently grouped.[71] The choice between systems is a function of problem-solving. The first option would work well in order to grasp a field as familiar and homogeneous as tonal music, since tonal (and even atonal and serial) works share many characteristics. To the contrary, in the attempt to organize a field as generally unfamiliar and heterogeneous as "sound art," the second option would seem more appropriate, since genres within this domain are determined by radically differing stylistic, performative and ontological characteristics. One temptation would be the non-categorical option of pure empiricism, which proffers a *sui generis* existence to every art work: no categories, only unique works. (Some even believe that not only does there exist no aesthetic *a priori*, but that every art work implies its own ontology.) If thought through categorically, such an empirical method would necessitate a sufficient number of characteristics per category so that in every case only one art work would correspond to a given category. This would, of course, effectively eliminate categories (which is why empiricism is the antithesis of structuralism). Such empiricism, while effective in focusing on individual works, would not be useful either in a comparative task or in organizing a field that is (albeit often illogically) divided into numerous domains, styles, and schools (variously and confusingly grouped according to aesthetic, structural, ontological, and sociological characteristics): sound art, sound poetry, concrete poetry, noise music, experimental music, aleatory music, Fluxus, etc. Perhaps, once the vast heterogeneity of the current field of sound art has been historically examined, and the structures of audio representation have become familiar, the provisional schema proposed below may be eliminated, and the empirical option finally adopted. But for the moment, categories are needed, even if only to reveal family resemblances between works, and to delineate different modes of representation.

The need for a comparative technique to determine the structures of audio representation provisionally suggests the value of a limited number of categories in binary opposition. In organizing this classificatory system, I would like to propose as a working hypothesis an *antinomy of classification*, where the terms are not pure limits, but interrelated polarities. Three of the major polarities within auditory mimesis — in terms of source, modality, and referentiality (respectively Aristotle's objects, means, imitations) — are constituted respectively by the differences between:

(A) *source*: concrete (recorded)/notated (performed)
(B) *modality*: hyperreal/stylized
(C) *referentiality*: evocative (simulation)/ambient (mood)

The various recombinations of these characteristics determine eight general categories of audio effects with their corresponding types of mimesis. The complexity of the categories resulting from this schema is in part due to the fact that the dimension of "source" is *ontological,* "modality" *aesthetic,* and "referentiality" *epistemological.* (One could of course multiply categories and add, for example, a *metaphysical* one to distinguish between real and imaginary referents. However, this would not only be too cumbersome, but would go beyond the heuristic needs of the present analysis. *This schema is a tool, not a reality check.*) Such categorizations and polarities will always be equivocal, precisely because of inevitable denotative and connotative differences between auditor responses. Consequently, this schematization must remain historicized by being constantly updated, until the moment when attunement to the differentiation between the microstructures of audio mimesis has become second nature, and the empirical option may be utilized.

(1) concrete/hyperreal/evocative
(2) concrete/hyperreal/ambient
(3) concrete/stylized/evocative
(4) concrete/stylized/ambient
(5) notated/hyperreal/evocative
(6) notated/hyperreal/ambient
(7) notated/stylized/evocative
(8) notated/stylized/ambient

It must be stressed that this schematization is in no way an attempt to totalize the field of the sound arts, and that the scope of this schema is conceived according to a historically limited sonic field: primarily that of

Western musics up until the digital era. It is intended as a tool for: (a) investigating the micro-structures of audiophonic representation; (b) offering precise descriptive possibilities of audio productions; (c) revising the study of auditory mimesis to reveal the inextricable relations between soundscape and landscape; (d) seeking a unified, though open-ended and provisional, field theory of the sound arts.[72] The term "concrete," derived from *musique concrète*, refers to recorded sound sources, which cannot (with certain exceptions) be notated — or to put it in other words, the real cannot be notated, except in its broadest features. The term "performed" signifies, in its largest scope, the non-concrete, and includes all sorts of performances susceptible to many types of notation, be it classic musical staffs and notes, marks on optical soundtracks, synthesizer keyboard sequences, IBM computer card punches, or the more contemporary keyboard strokes of computer sequencing, programming and sampling, as well as the binary encoding that now determines mathematically generated computer music. (Certain instruments, like the optical soundtrack, may serve both the concrete and the notated.) That many modern and contemporary musicians, especially in the varied improvisational traditions, have little interest in notation — whether or not their music can be notated — is besides the point in the present context, which deals with mimetic types of sound sources, not practical choices concerning notation. Synthesized sounds, for example, are often at the edge of notatability: when such novel sounds cannot be marked by classic musical notes, they can certainly be signified in terms of keystrokes — such complications reveal why this study deals mainly with the pre-digital era. To complicate matters even further, recorded elements are often used performatively — as in recordings that are recycled within other recordings or performances — through dubbing, sampling, remixing, turntablism, etc. Thus the concrete may indeed be notated, in form if not in content, though this is usually done in terms of use-value (noting tape length, tape speed, position in the mix, etc., or in digital form through equivalent numeric values). Such notation indicates aspects of the tape or the digital manipulation, not of the recorded event; and when the recorded event needs to be notated (as in certain instances of remixing musical segments in order to synchronize voices or establish harmonies), this is usually conceived according to semiotic, rather than musical, indications. For example, in remixing a recording of a Bach fugue, it suffices to indicate the part of the fugue in question; one need not have recourse to the sheet music to recopy the score, except in certain relatively rare instances, such as hybrid world-music superimpositions and mixes, where voices and instrumentals need be precisely aligned. Indeed, a single work of music may contain mimetic effects from varied combinations of categories — such as partially concrete and partially notated electroacoustic compositions — reassembled to create a symbolically overdetermined soundscape. While it is admittedly rather awkward to propose a set of categories that deconstruct as they are being conceived, I would again wish to stress that, complications and unwieldiness aside, *this analysis is not about musical styles, but mimetic forms.*

*

(1) Concrete/hyperreal/evocative. This is the category of maximal reality effect, and thus, strictly speaking, of the greatest documentary value, where the goal is to maintain the transparency of recording technology and montage techniques in order to establish the verisimilitude of a soundscape. It most clearly exemplifies the possibility of hearing the very sounds of the world as music. Yet the category of the "concrete" (recorded) is itself hybrid, since all performed sound — notated, unnotated, unnotatable — is inherently recordable, thus the "concrete" categories may certainly include notated and performed compositions.

Sometimes a single sound will produce an onomatopoetic-symbolic effect; sometimes an entire language is imbued with its riches. David Abram, in his philosophical study of ecology and magic, reveals the profound relations between sound, sense and site:

If we listen, first, to the sounds of an oral language — to the rhythms, tones and inflections that play through the speech of an oral culture — we will likely find that these elements are attuned, in multiple and subtle ways, to the contour and scale of the local landscape, to the depth of its valleys or the open stretch of its distances, to the visual rhythms of the local topography. But the human speaking is necessarily tuned, as well, to the various nonhuman calls and cries that animate the local terrain.[73]

Of course, these claims for the relations between speech and landscape in oral languages are equally true, *mutatis mutandis*, for written languages as well as for music. Witness, for example, the wondrous cosmogony expressed by Thoreau: "The sounds of peeping frogs (Hylodes) and dreaming toads are mingled into a sort of indistinct universal evening lullaby to creation, while the wind roars in the woods for a background or sea of sound, in which — on whose bosom — these others float."[74] In terms of music — in contrast to Messiaen's analytic abstraction of birdsong from the natural environment and its consequent transformation and stylization — one may point to the highly synthetic enterprise of Steven Feld's *Voices of the Rainforest* (1991), a syncretic work composed of numerous soundscape recordings including insect sounds, birdsong, and human chants, thus a typically hybrid work, since many parts of the recording contain performed and notated chants. Feld's composition-montage-mix offers the auditory evocation of a day in the lives of the Kaluli people of Papua New Guinea condensed into an hour-long audio mix. The aesthetic-epistemological premise of this recording, and of its corresponding discursive analysis, is that the music of the Kaluli is inseparable from their quotidian existence, and that this existence is further inseparable from the ecological totality of their landscape/soundscape.

To understand how Kaluli hear this world you have to get a handle on what they call dulugu ganalan, or "lift-up-over sounding." This refers to the fact that there are no single sounds in the rainforest. Everything is mixed into an interlocking soundscape. The rainforest is like a world of coordinated sound clocks, an intersection of millions of simultaneous cycles all refusing to ever start or stop at the same point. "Lift-up-over sounding" means that the Kaluli hear their rainforest world as overlapping, dense, layered. And they apply the same principle to their own music.[75]

Kaluli song and percussion are inspired by, and inextricably intertwined with, forest sounds: rain, wind, insects, water, and especially birdsong. The order — musical, existential, symbolic, mythic — within this extremely complex soundscape (a truly deep mix) is established through one specific mediation, that of birdsong, a reminder that the Kaluli are themselves an integral part of the forest. While they sing to nature, the forest also speaks and sings to them. Their entire symbolic system is mediated by birds, whose sounds — always understood as a dialogue between birds, humans, and the spirits of the dead — are categorized like Borges' Chinese encyclopedia: those who say their name; those who make a lot of noise; those who only sound; those who speak the Bosavi language (not unlike Thoreau's brown thrasher and veery speaking onomatopoeic English); those who whistle; those who weep; those who sing.[76] Analyzing Kaluli drumming, Feld explains:

Had we started with the dance we would have been led to bird mediation in the up/down movement and the image of a wokwele *at a waterfall. Had we concentrated on costuming, we would have been led to bird mediation in the symbolism of color. Had we begun with the larger sonic setting for drum performances in audience cheering and response, we would have been led to bird mediation in the way women's cheering is inspired by and patterned after the calls of the superb bird of paradise. Had we begun with staging, we would have been led to bird mediation in the concept of lighting the longhouse so that light splashes through the hall like the forest, lighting the birds that come and go and perch on their travels. Each feature of performance, context, staging, and sound leads back to this cen-*

tral notion: through the mediating scheme of bird transformation, Kaluli expressive behaviors are metaphorically empowered to communicate social ethos and emotion.[77]

The acoustic phenomenon of birdsong is experienced as part of a dense auditory matrix, mediated through a complex symbolic system, within which birdsong articulates the sundry aspects of Kaluli culture. Birdsong is heard both as part of the natural environment and the world of the spirit. These experiences should not appear as totally foreign to Western ears, for indeed, a central theme of mimetic theory is the origin of language: one common folk belief claims that human language originated in imitations of animal sounds, and that human music derived from onomatopoeic and vocalese versions of birdsong. It would seem that the Kaluli instantiate this theory.

The aesthetic dimension of Feld's recording implies a complex mediation between Kaluli rainforest acoustic ecology and the European ontology of sound reproduction. Current theorization has argued that recorded sound is not the simple copy of a sound, but rather, as Rick Altman explains, the *recording* of a *story* of a *sound event*, which reflexively bears traces of the recording and narrativizing processes: "To record is thus to recall to mind, as the dictionary would have it, but like most mnemonic devices, sound recordings must heighten some aspects of the original phenomenon at the expense of others. So-called recordings are thus always representations, interpretations, partial narratives that must nevertheless serve as our only access to the sounds of the past."[78] The ontological complications of this theoretical position may be schematized by the declension inherent in the subchapters of his seminal article, "The Material Heterogeneity of Recorded Sound": Sound Events: The Production of Sound — The Sound Narrative: The Story of a Sound Event — The Sound Record: Recording the Story of a Sound Event — Sound Reproduction: Playing the Record of the Story of a Sound Event — Hearing Events: Hearing the Record of the Story of a Sound Event — Sound Terminology: Talking about Hearing the Record of the Story of a Sound Event.[79] (The latter is precisely what I am doing here.) It is for reasons based on this schema that I suggest "hyperreal" rather than "real" in the present schematization of mimetic musical types. The fact that all recorded music is necessarily a construction implies that technological means of representation transform the ontology of the real, and that this ontology is constituted by numerous representational layers, related not only by correspondence but also by contradiction. What appears as real is always a palimpsest of effects and forms, of causes and effects, a dense web of significations well beyond conscious expectations and predictions.

Sound recording simultaneously re-produces and re-presents. This, however, does not obviate the hyperbolically mimetic faculties of sound recording — "Is it real, or is it Memorex?" — the *bête noire* of anti-ideology critique. Rather, it reveals that the mimetic functions of any medium are always mediated by the symbolic matrix in which it operates, as Bachelard has shown regarding onomatopoeia, and as Messiaen, Feld, and the Kaluli have revealed regarding the relation between human song and birdsong. Indeed, the *trompe-l'oreille* powers of mimesis are not to be denied, as Feld points out regarding one delicate moment of his research. In order to obtain high quality recordings of the very shy birds, he first recorded the reluctant bird-in-question at a distance and then played back the recording in order to attract the very same bird with its own voice, so as to better record it close-up. He describes the techniques involved in this endeavor:

> *I developed the playback technique in the 80s, working in trees and bird blinds. I would record a bird of the mid canopy or lower reaches or mid distant ground and then rewind the Nagra and instantly play back the recording, loud, almost distorted, through a 1 dollar Radio Shack speaker. This had the effect of holding a mirror up to the bird. As a result the bird would, in time, come closer, interested but confused by this instant playback of its own voice. After hours or days or weeks I was then able to record various birds relatively close up, the way I could record a person. For this reason I never used parabolic reflectors or shotgun mics, just very sensitive cardioid*

capsules (AKG 451B + CK1). When I recorded Voices of the Rainforest *in 1990 I used this technique, and then in the studio we made samples of about 20 key bird calls from the close ups. Then in the multitrack mix we would listen for the more distant presence of a bird in the guide or real-time track, and add a sampled layer, on top of the original, of the same bird's voice with a closeup recording. This made it possible to recreate more of the acoustic height and depth layers of the forest in multitrack, without ever using parabolic or hypercardioid technologies, just simple AB or XY stereo, in 3 or 4 multitrack layers. The result, obviously, is an acoustic hyper-realism. That is the defining aesthetic of* Voices of the Rainforest, *and it is that kind of hyper-realism that makes it possible for people to instantly hear the kinds of spatial and temporal subtleties and nuances that took me years to learn to hear. In a sense the naive listener to that recording just acoustically leaps over numerous auditory hurdles that I stumbled on and around for the 15 years of research I did in Bosavi before I came to make that CD. What I still love most about* Voices of the Rainforest *is the way people can quickly experience a kind of acoustic intimacy that would otherwise require years of listening and research.*[80]

This explanation is a wonderful allegory of the assymmetry between mimesis in the human and animal domains. While years of work and very sophisticated recording and mixing technologies are necessary to attain the "Memorex effect" for humans, a quick recording and a $1 speaker suffice in the ornithological realm. Should we assume that birds are ideologically naive creatures? That said, it is also the case that certain birds can recognize (appreciate?) human music, as Don Stap notes: "Pigeons, for instance, have been invited to listen to excerpts from both Bach's *Toccata and Fugue in D Minor* and *Toccata and Fugue in F* for organ and Stravinsky's *Rite of Spring* for orchestra. And it turns out that some pigeons can distinguish between the two composers 90 percent of the time. They also 'classified' Bach, Stravinsky, and several other composers in much the same way as human subjects did in the same test."[81]

In any case, technical decisions in recording are always aesthetic and symbolic choices. Paradigmatic is the technical conundrum in recording orchestras: whether to simply set up a stereo microphone in the acoustic center of the concert hall, or to use numerous microphones to capture individual instruments and instrument groups. The latter solution permits bringing up certain instruments in the mix so as to overcompensate for the loss of visual cues (to accentuate solos, for example), but it also occasionally produces aberrations, such as a flute sounding louder than an entire orchestra.[82] Feld recognized the complexity of these exigencies in producing *Voices of the Rainforest*, whence its hyperrealism. Instead of presenting a real-time stereo recording of the environment, the different acoustic parts of the forest were broken down into individual recordings (with the acoustic textures and density of the rainforest enhanced by a mix of 75 different individually recorded bird, frog, insect and human voices), and later remixed according to suggestions by the Kaluli themselves. Especially important are the spatial imaging techniques used in the mixing, since the actual decibel level of the birdsong was relatively low in relation to the totality of forest sounds, while its high symbolic value demanded particular attention. In order to create a soundscape congruent with Kaluli perception, imagination and symbolism, the birdsong needed to be foregrounded in the mix.[83] Whence the need to accentuate certain birdsongs, as well as to enhance the background sounds with sampled doubles of the foregrounded birds. Mimesis is heightened according to symbolic mediation, and as each sonic part echoes with the totality of the environment, music is meaningfully linked to ecology.

*

(2) Concrete / hyperreal / ambient. Of all the postulated categories, this is — along with "notated / hyperreal / ambient" category — perhaps the most abstruse: the hyperbolic representation of a diffuse, often ill-defined, soundscape.[84] Figure and ground are confounded, such that the original re-

corded sources (of either details of sonic events or even entire sonic environments) become unrecognizable when abstracted into musical form, resulting in a diffuse ambience. Though based on recordings, their referent is often indeterminable, and in most cases cannot be grasped without supporting documentation. This obtains both because the experience of ambience is here organized at the extreme lower limit of representation (minimal evocation), and because these recordings correspond to phenomena that are in themselves often rare or arcane (unfamiliar denotation). Such works are farthest from both theoretical and popular conceptions of music, and are often unrecognizable as music per se. Consider Alvin Lucier's *Sferics*, a recording from midnight to dawn on 27 August 1981 made with home-made antennas that serve to capture sferics, or whistlers, which are natural radio-frequencies in the ionosphere caused by electromagnetic energy generated by lightning. Every once in a while a very slight *hiss* or *zip* is heard on the record (please excuse the paucity of the onomatopocia in this instance), sounds which may well be mistaken by the listener for mere surface noise on the original analogue vinyl disks. The musicological interest of these recordings resides in both the curiosity of this natural phenomenon (verging on scientific documentary or science-fiction effects rather than music), and in the current fascination with what John Cage termed "small sounds," those needing microphones in order to be captured and amplification to be heard. *Sferics* would seem to set the miminal conditions for concrete music.

Perhaps a more pertinent musical example within this category would be Iannis Xenakis' *Concret PH* (1958) — composed for Le Corbusier's Philips Pavilion (designed for the most part by Xenakis) at the 1958 Brussels World's Fair, and named for the hyperbolic paraboloid forms (PH) that constitute the architectural design.[85] *Concret PH* was intended as acoustic "filler" between auditions of Edgar Varèse's *Poème électronique* (the name given to both the entirety of Le Corbusier's project and more specifically to Varèse's musical composition which was part of the pavilion's sound-and-image show), and is based on the recorded and electronically transformed sounds of burning charcoal, with its characteristic tingling sheet of sound. This piece is emblematic of Xenakis' 1950s musical research on stochastics (mass statistical structures), such as the chirping of crickets or the patter of rain. With historic and musicological retrospect, one might well consider *Concret PH* a more seminal work than the *Poème électronique*: the minimalism, formalism and indeterminism of the former make it a harbinger of so much to come, while the latter seems to remain fixed in an antiquated fantasy of electronic music. Varèse, while composing works such as *Ionisation* (1931), dreamt of circumventing the limitations of the twelve tones of the chromatic scale, expanding the range of timbre by introducing noise into music, and freeing rhythm from regular meter – a musical project necessitating machines that would permit the creation of any sound the composer could imagine. The irony is that while *Ionisation* was the harbinger of a rich sonic future, a mere quarter century later he seemed locked into his own past, unable to tease the forms and push the limits of the burgeoning electronic field. For by the time he was confronted with one of the first synthesizing electronic devices in 1956 for the creation of the *Poème électronique* (concrete/hyperreal/evocative), the musical composition that resulted was already obsolete: more a paratactically organized, programmatic compendium of preconceived effects (vaguely cued to the corresponding film that covered the wall of the pavilion) than an investigation of the radical potential of such new technologies. To the contrary, Xenakis immediately grasped that a most convincing way of dealing with the infinite possibilities of recorded sounds (noises) was by intense selectivity of sound coupled with rigorous imposition of structure, in this case the radically innovative use of mathematical models for musical composition. (The use of non-musical compositional models – of which one of the earliest examples is Erik Satie's use of cinematographic editing forms corresponding to the abrupt transitions between sections in the music for René Clair's film, *Entr'acte cinématographique* from the ballet *Relâche* (1924) – has become common avant-garde practice.)[86]

Xenakis' architectural design for the Philips Pavilion, consisting primarily of hyperbolic parabolas, was directly inspired by the glissandi of two of his earlier compositions: *Metastasis* (1954), a piece for 61 instruments (strings, trombones, percussion) playing 61 separate parts mainly composed of glissandi, an homage to Varèse's earlier works; and *Pithoprakta* (1956), a stochastic work for 46 strings, 2 trombones, 1 xylophone and 1 wood block, contrasting continuity and discontinuity, glissandi and pizzicati. However, his musical composition for the Philips Pavilion, *Concret PH*, had no discernible structural relation to either the architecture or to Varèse's music: it is a work of ontological equivocation, given the impossibility of determining whether it is abstract or programmatic.

In a certain sense, *La légende d'Eer* — the sound component of the *Diatope* (1977-78) — constituted Xenakis' answer to the limitations of the music and architecture of the *Poème électronique*.[87] As we shall see, with *La légende d'Eer* (notated /hyperreal /ambient) there is no such equivocation, since the project for the *Diatope* was conceived as a unified whole, where the music is fully integrated with the architecture and abstract laser light show. Its program — a not so veiled critique of the egocentric humanism of the Philips Pavilion — is totally determinate, contrasting hell on earth and the rule of the aleatory to Le Corbusier's and Varèse's humanistic, utopian formalism.

*

(3) Concrete /stylized /evocative. This category is perhaps most commonly identified with conceptualized manipulation of the material specificity of the tape — whether magnetic sound recording tape or optical tracks on film stock — utilizing high modernist techniques such as montage, micromontage, phasing, tape reversal, tape speed variation, amplification of noise, etc. Compare, for example, Cage's micromontage of *Williams Mix* (1952) with Robert Breer's single frame editing of the same period in *Recreation* (1956); or the editing techniques of Steve Reich's *It's Gonna Rain* (1965) with the contemporaneous films of Paul Sharits such as

N:O:T:H:I:N:G (1968) and *T,O,U,C,H,I,N,G* (1968), where the very punctuation in the titles alludes to the radical mode of editing.[88]

The reconception of spatiality as a function of montage was already fantasized at least as early as Guillaume Apollinaire's 1916 tale *Le Roi-Lune* [The Moon-King] from his anthology *Le Poète assassiné* [The Assassinated Poet]. The narrator, who loses his path in a storm, takes refuge in a cave, where, in its depths, he discovers the underground domain of the still living mad King Ludwig II of Bavaria. In these caverns, decorated with ancient graffiti evoking an "anachronistic orgy" suggesting "voluptuousness in the arms of death," the narrator found Ludwig seated at the keyboard of a pipe-organ that turned out to be of universal proportions. For, with the aid of sensitive microphones placed at strategic positions around the world, the musician could play a symphony composed of a sort of *musique concrète*: Japan at dawn, geysers in a New Zealand morning, a market in Tahiti, voices in China, a train in the American plains, streets of Chicago at noon, boats on the Hudson River in New York, violent prayers in Mexico City, a carnivalesque cavalcade in Rio de Janeiro, evening songs in Martinique, a café in Paris, the sounds of the angelus in Münster and Bonn, a boat on the Rhine arriving in Coblenz, nighttime in Naples, a bivouac in Tripolitania, voices in Isfahan, midnight in an Asian desert, the sound of elephants at one o'clock in the morning in India, sacerdotal bells in Tibet, barques on the river in Saigon, gongs and drums in Peking, the sound of a rooster announcing dawn in Korea. "The king's fingers ran across the keyboard at random, causing to resound, simultaneously as it were, all the noises of this world around which we had just made an immobile, auricular voyage."[89] After this recital, in a somewhat anachronistic bow to the composer's modernism, the King demanded the score of Wagner's *Rheingold*. The sonorous world is sampled and recombined, and we can well imagine the sounds of this world set to an infinite Wagnerian backbeat in a masterpiece of dub abstraction. The epitome of the world-encompassing *Gesamtkunstwerk* is Alexander Scriabin's project — certainly more accurately referred to as a fantasy, or even a delusion — *The Prefatory Act*, conceived in 1913, which would be a truly total art work, far surpassing anything proposed by Wagner, combining music, dance, drama, fireworks, light effects, pillars of incense, disparate temples, even dreams. Indeed, even the contrapuntal relations of clouds and wind, and the antiphonal correlation of sun and moon, would take part, literally making of it a cosmic work. The performance would culminate in the finale of the *Mysterium*, an apocalyptic moment in which all participants dissolve in an ethereal whirlwind and join in an ecstasy of illumination signalling the destruction of the universe.[90] Any genealogy of contemporary ambient music and soundscapes would need to consider these antecedents.

Filmmaker Hollis Frampton claims that "a still photograph is simply an isolated frame taken out of the infinite cinema."[91] What if we were to think of music and sound art in the same manner? Though John Cage created an early series of works entitled *Imaginary Landscape*, his most influential composition in the domain of soundscapes (auditory landscapes) is his famed *Williams Mix*, a micromontage of hundreds of bits of tape from a stock of 600 recordings, mixing city sounds, country sounds, electronic sounds, manually produced sounds (including music), wind produced sounds (including song), and small sounds (needing amplification), all chance-organized and spliced into one-second segments. The radical heterogeneity of space and time is as ancient as art itself, and we find self-conscious instantiations of such hybridization at least as early as Francesco Colonna's curious book, *Hypnerotomachia Poliphili* (1499), one of the sources of imagining the garden as a heterogeneous site. Contemporaneous with the development of the realist novel as the literary form that includes all other literary forms, certain gardens at the origins of modernity, such as Les Buttes-Chaumont in 19th century Paris — a pastiche mixing formal and informal; Chinese, English and French; picturesque and urban styles — offered prime sites of experimentation with formal heterogeneity.[92] Indeed, an investigation of all art forms will certainly reveal the temptation of the hybrid. While music occasionally evokes heterogeneous spaces, as in Milhaud and Ives, audio art needed to await the invention of magnetic recording tape and the advent of *musique concrète* to fully realize such hybrid potentials. In a strange sense, *Williams Mix* is a programmatic (*i.e.*, narrative) work of music, but the tale it tells is of the radical heterogeneity of representational space and the polyrhythmic temporality of events. While most music, however polyrhythmic, is nevertheless temporally abstract and reductive, *Williams Mix* opens the musical domain to the infinitude of worldly rhythms (events). As such, it should be considered in the lineage of subsequent deconstructive investigations of the modernist landscape, such as Situationist psychogeography and Robert Smithson's *non-sites*, where spatial representation and referentiality are overdetermined as malleable and mobile, susceptible to synecdochic condensation and hyperbolic mont-age.[93] Needless to say, these considerations should in turn inform and inspire the study of site-specific sound installations, whether in landscape, cityscape, or gallery settings. Furthermore, an integral, indeed essential, aspect of the use-value of recording technologies entails the entry of the aleatory into artistic production. While conception, notation and gesture are sources of control in creation and performance, recording (whether photographic or phonographic) is a source of chance appearances and events, since however controlled the situation, the recorded event or site is imbued with details which escape the control of the recordist or artist. Such aleatory detail is at the core of modernist aesthetics.[94]

In *Williams Mix*, the very transformation of rhythm is central to the critique of representation. In the late 1940s, Cage realized that rhythm need not be bound to metrics (*i.e.*, to a sense of temporal regularity): "rhythm is not at all something periodic and repetitive. It is the fact that something happens, something unexpected, something *irrelevant*."[95] Rhythm, in its broadest definition, is the temporal relation between any two sound events whatsoever (no matter how many other sounds, or how much silence, or how much time or space, intervenes between the two.) Rhythm has to do with framing rather than counting. *Williams Mix* creates a new sort of polyrhythm, where the mathematically regular metrics of the tape montage – with its apparent 1/1 beat of one-second segments – is in stark contrast

to the nearly infinite scope of the microrhythms *within* the one-second
segments, determined by the sundry, aleatory events of the recordings. In
this context, *Williams Mix* is not so much polyrhythmic as *heterorhythmic*:
the metric scansion of the one-second segments is a montage device that
establishes a surreal articulation of disparate sites and sounds, each with
its own internal rhythm and external referential scope.

Only recently has such a notion of temporality been applied to issues
of landscape, as in the extraordinary reading of the irregular wave patterns
on 6th century B.C. Ionico-Massalian pottery offered by Gustaf Sobin
in *Luminous Debris*. These waves represent an originary organic rhythm,
before rationalizing Greek thought would regulate motion by transmuting
it into cadence, meter, "good form." The rhythm of these waves — before
Logos succumbed to the rule of Eidos — reveals "the fluid architecture of
each given instance," a rhythm characterized as, "an iridescent chaos, as
Cézanne once put it: a place from which the virginity of the world might, once
again, be experienced."[96] Such quasi-musical investigations of visualized
rhythm are invaluable for expanding research on the representational
implications of music, and suggest elaborations and transformations of
rhythm in aleatory, concrete, electronic and digital music. No longer can
the representation of landscape be conceived as a stable "picture," as it
was for so many centuries. For not only is growth the essence of gardens,
but catastrophic destruction is also essential to their very being. All the
chaos of corporeal movement and natural growth (as well as decay and
apocalypse) are at the horizon of such representations.

*

(4) Concrete/stylized/ambient. This category, of nebulous referentiality, is perhaps best characterized by the term *Stimmung*, taken in its
broadest lexical scope: in the musical sense of tuning, key, pitch; the psychological sense of mood, temper, state of mind; and the existential sense
of atmosphere, ambience, impression. Its effects are often associated with

the seemingly antipodal styles of New Age music and Noise Music, but are hardly limited to such.

Scott Konzelmann's *Dry Hole* (1997) a work of "noise music" of extreme rigor and minimalism, is part of *Psychogeographical Dip* (1997), a CD project organized by Geoff Dugan and inspired by Situationist psychogeography, evoking and celebrating the space of the abandoned McCarren Park Pool in Greenpoint, Brooklyn. In answer to some technical questions about *Dry Hole*, Konzelmann responded with the following:

Dry Hole — *Of course, no Lewis Carroll reference is implied!!! That's way too easy. I titled it not so much as an application simply to the pool site concept of the compilation, but as my entire body of work can perhaps be best described as placing one's ear to a disturbed and convulsive hole in the ground. That statement reflects my overall approach — to draw the listener's attention to smaller, odd sounds normally dismissed or not heard by the unobservant listener — then, to literally PULL the listener inside them. Envelope, immerse. Same approach holds for my equal obsession with distant sounds — I want the listener to concentrate focus and be drawn to them, as I am. Even if the original sound is one that is quite loud and easily identified, I try to distill its particular internal elements that strike my ear and focus them. All of my sound material at its core develops from carefully captured field recordings, or further controlled playback of those primary sound materials through my "Speaker Constructions" (sculptural assemblages incorporating loudspeakers). My further distillations, or processes, are very simple — and purely analog. Funny, I do feel the need these days to stress that I firmly remain adherent to the analog format — not as a "stance" or position, but that it's an integral element in the development and the character of my "sound," and how I hear it, approach it, and work with it. Analog lends a "precarious" tonal quality to my presentations, and also often allows for "the happy accident" — something other manifests and imprints itself on tape that was not at all prepared or planned for. I let the process unfold, I just try to steer it as it develops and presents its poten-*

tial elements to my ears. I do not discount the prevalent digital world and its possibilities out of hand, I simply don't use it. For me — its proper and improvised microphone techniques used in all stages of capture, the use of magnetic tape — and utilizing the tape recorders as the instruments so to speak — as the medium to build what I consider the "organic" mutation of the initial source material — with additional playback filtering, equalization, manipulation of tape speeds, and layering to tailor the materials, leading to the final capture recording. One could of course call me on that the majority of my material originates from man-made machines and activities. I do, however, consider it to be organic in the sense that these sounds are truly a part of our sonic landscape. There is also something to be said for my fragmenting them and making sources unrecognizable to perhaps address them, as well as the use of the speaker constructions — ventriloquy![97]

Dry Hole (and the entire "concrete /stylized /ambient" category) points to the contemporary equivocation between the terms "music," "sound art" and "noise music" (or simply "noise"), suggesting that perhaps they need be considered within a single sonic spectrum under a less historically loaded heading. Konzelmann proposes the term "structured" or "focused" noise (harkening back to Cage's notion of music as "organized noise") as providing a satisfactory classification of his work.[98] He ultimately insists that the simple terms "sound" or "noise" should suffice. Perhaps we might use the neutral "sound art," or simply "audio," as the title of this book suggests. In any case, to answer such questions, it would be useful to suggest several possible paths towards a genealogy of works such as *Dry Hole*, with their radical transformation (and often dissimulation) of ambient sounds.

(a) *Echo and reverb effects.* In part due to a fascination with canon, and in part for the pleasures of *trompe l'oreille*, the Baroque was fascinated with echo effects. One of the most famous is heard in Gregorio Allegri's *Miserere* (c. 1638), a sublime moment created by having the end of a phrase sung by a soprano (or in Allegri's time, a castrato) in front of the choir repeated by a second singer behind the choir, as in echo. A more contemporary example is Paul Horn's and Pauline Oliveros' site-specific improvisational investigations of extreme acoustic spaces, such as the inside of the pyramids and Cistercian reservoirs. Most astounding is the Taj Mahal, which has a 28 second decay time, such that Horn discovered that a short melodic riff would return as a chord; and the Fort Worden Cistern in Port Townsend, Washington, where Pauline Oliveros recorded *Deep Listening* (1988), of which she wrote concerning the 45 second reverberation:

> *The sound is so well mirrored, so to speak, that it's hard to tell direct sound from the reflective sound. It puts you in the deep listening space. You're hearing the past, of the sound you made; you're continuing it, possibly, so you're right in the present, and you're anticipating the future, which is coming at you from the past…. So it puts you into the simultaneity of time, which is quite wonderful, but it's challenging to maintain it and stay concentrated…. The space itself becomes a very active partner in the creation but how you listen to it is how it gets shaped.*[99]

Another interesting example exists in the Ludwigsburg Castle in Germany, where a painted eagle adorns the top of the cupola: the acoustics are such that the rapidly succeeding echoes of a handclap from directly underneath sound like the flapping of wings.

In this context, Alvin Lucier's famed *I Am Sitting in a Room* (1969) — where a brief discourse is played back between two tape recorders over and over in a room such that the sound is distorted and transformed by the specific acoustics of the space, to finally "disintegrate" into a beautiful three note melody — has become paradigmatic in illustrating the decay of sound. One expects the speech to decompose into sheer noise, yet the decreasing verisimilitude and comprehensibility coincides with a surprising proportionally increasing musicality. Gregory Whitehead's brilliant spoof of the piece, *The William S. Burroughs Tape Worm Mutation* (1991), should be reckoned with in this context. Here, Whitehead performs, before a live audience, the *imagined* results of recording and rerecording in Lucier's manner the sentence, "I am a degenerate," 17, 42, 93, 152, and 327 times.

Extrapolating the final degeneration, this elegant pastiche results in precisely the opposite of Lucier's equally elegant experiment: a sound that Whitehead characterizes (inspired by Edgar Allan Poe's *The Facts in the Case of M. Valdemar*) as the "vile putresence" of inarticulate noise. Whitehead comments on the piece:

> *The words pass from mouth to ear to another mouth and another ear, and with each passing, they receive another generation of digestion. Words, eaten, or sometimes just stuffed, and somewhere down there, the stomach churns and boils, along with the badinage. On the other side of the dark acid, further down, a tape worm languishes, waiting to get fed; a tape worm whose appetite knows no limit, a tape worm who wishes to digest the whole host. A tape worm that wants, in fact, to be a tongue "an sich." Analog technologies know all this — that's what makes them analogous. They know we are degenerates, with every utterance, and every discourse. It all goes in circles, and the circle is degenerative (even more so when properly needled), and the end is grease, or mud, or miasma. In the digital universe, all this is numbered and hidden. But the truth still comes out, because the worm is not so easily fooled. I am happy to tell you who I am, but the worm will tell you where I go, and where I end. Listen, and repeat!*[100]

One should note the explicit valorization of analogue reproduction, essential to contemporary audio creativity precisely because of the "parasites" (as the French call static) that inhabit it.

(b) *Serendipity.* This is a subcategory of the aleatory. The history of technical recording errors constitutes a curious footnote to the genealogy of audiophonic creativity. Even though certain serendipitous effects lead to no immediate innovations, creative or technological, they do nevertheless suggest fields of future investigation by revealing what was sonically possible (however marginal) in a given epoch.[101] Three such examples might well make the case. First, during a 1947 recording session that included the bebop tune *Crazyology* performed by Charlie Parker and J. J. Johnson, a technical error caused the tune to be recorded with dub delay refraction (a slightly unsynchronized double feed onto the cutting lathe), which created a distinct and unintended reverb effect. The discrepancy was such that the effect went far beyond a simulated echo, and suggested reverb techniques that would subsequently become a staple of rock guitar. Second, during the famed *Jazz at Massey Hall* concert (1953), the bass of leader Charles Mingus was improperly miked. He consequently overdubbed a bass line in the studio, the result of which was that in the quieter moments of the bass solos, especially on the tune *All the Things You Are*, one can distinctly hear not only two nearly simultaneous bass lines in the form of a sort of canon, but even more astoundingly, Mingus appears to be soloing with himself. The third example requires a bit of humility. In a study of Luis Buñuel's film *L'Âge d'Or*, I cleverly interpreted the founding of Rome speech — incomprehensible babble except for the single phrase "*les matières primaires elles-mêmes*" [prime matter itself] — as linking the origins of language (glossolalia, babble) with the origins of sculpture symbolized by the scatological images (*matière primaire*, prime matter, excrement) which appear at that point of the film.[102] Years later, I was asked to present the digitalized version of the film in the series *Un dimanche, une oeuvre* at the Centre Pompidou/IRCAM. After my presentation, glossolalia and all, the beautifully remastered film was screened, and to my great humiliation, the glossolalia was no such thing. The entire speech was intelligible, if fuzzy, consisting of a text on the prime matter used in ceramics. The "glossolalia" was an effect of inadequate technology, not poetic justice.

(c) *Minimalism.* Here I would like to propose an emblematic tale of two notes. The title tune of the Jimmy Smith record *Open House* (1960) is a blues jam that culminates in an organ solo by the leader, the first jazz virtuoso on the Hammond B-3 organ, followed by a guitar solo by Quentin Warren. After his solo, Smith holds a single C (blues F) note through the melodic line of the guitar solo for approximately 25 bars (an organ technique termed pedal-point for low notes and inverted pedal for high notes), a sort of drone around which the melody is played. This was probably the longest note performed in jazz up to that time. Yet, however virtuosic the solo, sustaining that note offered no difficulty whatsoever: due to the magic of electronics, the mere touch of a single finger sufficed. In stark contrast, at around the same time, Tony Conrad was beginning his experiments in minimalism and his investigations into harmonics. In 1962 he introduced the sustained drone of just intonation into Western modernist music, culminating in *Four Violins* (1964), a solo four-track overdub in which the musical task was to hold a single note on the violin for as long and as perfectly as possible, over and over, without faltering. The gesture was virtuosic, even if the results were seemingly basic and hyperbolically minimal. While pushing violin technique to certain limits, the goal — a sustained perfect note — was to concentrate on the harmonics, to hear the *inside* of the note (as Konzelmann and others would later do with recorded sounds). This structural intuition seeks to delineate the differences *within* notes (harmonics) rather than the differences *between* notes (intervals). Conrad was variously influenced by Heinrich Biber's *Mystery Sonatas* (where the violin is tuned differently for each piece), the role of the drone in Indian music, John Cage's fascination with "small sounds," and La Monte Young's minimalism, which led to the following realization:

> *Pitched pulses, palpitating beyond rhythm and cascading the cochlea with a galaxy of synchronized partials, reopen the awareness of the sine tone — the element of combinatorial hearing. Together and in pairs in all combinations, the partials combine. The ear responds uniquely. We lived inside the sound, for years. As our precision increased, almost infinitesimal pitch changes became glaring smears across the surface of the sound.*[103]

The goal was to expand and refine the lower threshold of auditory perception, a task radically simplified with the advent of digital analysis and synthesis. In a word, the result was the antithesis of Jimmy Smith's beautiful long note. Such investigations of microtonality are not unrelated to György Ligeti's contemporaneous attempt to create a sonorous continuum at the limits of auditory perception through an exploration of micropolyphony and microharmony in pieces such as *Apparitions* (1959) and *Atmos-*

phères (1961) — works without melody, composed of shifting transformations of tone color and dynamics. In all such cases, we shall recognize in the "smears" of the miniature sine tone glissandi or slippage a "fault" at the core of musical sound that resonates from Busoni through Xenakis as an emblem of modernist audiophony.

*

(5) Notated/hyperreal/evocative. This category consists of musical mimesis in the most common sense of the term, and as such it encompasses many effects of programmatic music. (We shall see that the "notated/hyperreal/evocative" category is closely linked to, and often indistinguishable from, the "notated/stylized/evocative" category.) It also includes a narrower and rare type of mimesis, where one form of music is imitated by another. For example, the relatively simple birdcall transpositions in Messiaen's compositions, or the exceedingly complex transcription of Brian Eno's electronic *Music for Airports* scored for electric and acoustic instruments by the Bang on a Can Allstars. The mimetic relations between performed and concrete music are in fact reciprocal though asymmetrical: a given concrete effect may often (though certainly not always) be transposed into performed music, and of course any performance of notated music whatsoever may be recorded, thus "concretized," and consequently made ready for sampling, transposition, remixing.

Film theorist and historian David Bordwell relates the anecdote that while staying at the house of a friend who had a parrot, for several days he couldn't understand why the tea-kettle always whistled a few seconds before it began to boil, until he realized that what he heard wasn't the kettle, but the parrot anticipating the whistling kettle. On a more poetic note, Yasunari Kawabata offers the following scene in *Snow Country*: "The innkeeper had lent him an old Kyoto teakettle, skillfully inlaid in silver with flowers and birds, and from it came the sound of wind in the pines. He could make out two pine breezes, as a matter of fact, a near one and a far one. Just beyond the far breeze he heard faintly the tinkling of a bell."[104] This passage recalls (and might well be based on) another, from Kakuzo Okakura's classic, *The Book of Tea*: "The kettle sings well, for pieces of iron are so arranged in the bottom as to produce a peculiar melody in which one may hear the echoes of a cataract muffled by clouds, of a distant sea breaking among the rocks, a rainstorm sweeping through a bamboo forest, or of the soughing of pines on some faraway hill."[105] All Japanese poetics depends upon such sonic correspondences: we conceive the kettle as both instrument and synthesizer, listening for the mimetic music of the world.

Here we enter the realm of mimesis proper, long an incidental feature of Western music, most often relegated to programmatic music and the sonic gags of popular entertainment. Thoreau's mockingbird, Bras' gargouillou, and Goethe's nymphs would fall into this category, and Western music abounds in such effects. Wagner's *Ring* cycle, for example, teems with such mimetic instances, and many leitmotifs are inspired by specific mimetic forms, such as the clanging sound of hammer and anvil during the scene of the forging of the sword in *Siegfried* (1856). Compare the pealing of church bells and the discharges of cannons in the finale of Pyotr Tchaikovsky's *1812 Overture* (1880); the feeble syncopated rhythm of the opening strains of Gustav Mahler's *Ninth Symphony* (1910), echoing the arythmia of his heart; the imitation of the sounds of a moving train in Arthur Honegger's *Pacific 231* (1923), more famously reproduced in Duke Ellington's renditions of Billy Strayhorn's *Take the A Train* (1941); the "sneeze" that begins Zoltán Kodály's *Háry János Suite* (1925-6); the entire orchestra imitating the tones of a pipe organ behind the choir in the *Exaudi orationem meam, Domina* of Igor Stravinsky's *Symphony of Psalms* (1948); the sounds of city traffic in the opening section of Bud Powell's *Parisian Thoroughfare* (1951), and the even more emphatically mimetic version of traffic in George and Ira Gershwin's *A Foggy Day* as performed on Charles Mingus' *Pithecanthropus Erectus* album (1956), with its whistles, sirens and honks suggesting a congested street scene; or the extraordinary imitation of a transistor radio being tuned in Vocal Sampling's version of René Baños' *Radio Reloj* (1995). This latter effect recalls the fact that the onomatopoeic reproduction of radiophonic sounds was an integral part of early modernist poetry, most notably the case in Guillaume Apollinaire's poem "Lettre-Océan" from *Les soirées de Paris* (1914), and in Mexican avant-garde poet Kyn Taniya's poem "IU IIIUUU IU" (1924), the title itself being an onomatopoeia for the tuning of a radio.[106] Perhaps uncanniest of all is the electronic imitation of the human voice singing arias on the Theremin, that early electronic instrument almost exclusively devoted to glissandi. In such renditions, the extreme effects of vocalese are effectively imitated, and the saccharin borders on the uncanny as human is replaced by machine. John Cage offered a pointed critique of such musical curiosities:

> *When Theremin provided an instrument with genuinely new possibilities, Thereministes did their utmost to make the instrument sound like some old instrument, giving it a sickeningly sweet vibrato, and performing upon it, with difficulty, masterpieces from the past. Although the instrument is capable of a wide variety of sound qualities, obtained by the turning of a dial, Thereministes act as censors, giving the public those sounds they think the public will like. We are shielded from new sound experiences.*[107]

This, alas, remained true for nearly two decades, with several notable exceptions, such as the use of the Ondes Martenot (a Theremin-like instrument) in Olivier Messiaen's *Turangalîla-Symphonie* (1948). Yet it was the science-fiction film, and not concert music, that liberated such electronic instruments from an all-too-conventional usage, notably the orchestra containing two Theremins, two Hammond organs, and electrically amplified instruments used in Bernard Hermann's score for *The Day the Earth Stood Still* (1951), which remains a paradigm of sci-fi music and sound effects.

All of the above are, however, minor instances of instrumental mimesis when compared to the effects of the pipe organ, the mimetic instrument *par excellence*, often referred to as the first musical synthesizer. Perusal of the vast list of stops of the organ at the Atlantic City Convention Hall (though not fully functional, it is nevertheless the largest in the world, with 33,112

pipes in 455 ranks; 1,439 stop keys; 1,255 speaking stops; 7 manuals)
bears out this imitative musical imperative: fife, concert flute, brass cornet,
clarinet, bassett horn, cor anglais, trumpet, harp, saxophone, xylophone,
chimes, cymbal, carillon, drums, violin, cello, tuba maxima, etc. In short,
this organ can synthesize most sounds of the Western musical universe,
from the earthly *vox humana* all the way to the *vox caelestis* of the angels.
(However, I have yet to discover an organ stop for the *vox diabolicus*.)

In this regard, one of the great curiosities in the history of musical
mimesis is György Ligeti's *Study for Organ: #1 Harmonies* (1967), a beautiful,
haunting work of the most subtle nuances, truly in a class by itself. This
nearly static piece consists of the extremely slow, almost excruciatingly
subtle transformation of a single harmony: 231 chords composed of 10 notes
apiece, each differing from the other by a single finger movement resulting
in a continual semi-tone transition, linked with the extended technique of
reduced wind pressure that causes constantly wavering pitch. The result
is that a standard pipe organ is made to imitate the sounds of electronic
instruments, a mimesis of the most unusual sort.[108]

*

(6) Notated/hyperreal/ambient. This is an extremely complex category, most radical in terms of its implications for the constitution of imaginary landscapes and the elaboration of a philosophy of the imagination.
Here, the hyperreal referent is not a singular recognizable sound event (as
is the case of the "notated/hyperreal/evocative" category), but the evocation of an entire nebulous, inchoate environment. Wagner's last oper-
as, for example, fall into this category: the all-encompassing presence of
ever-changing and ceaselessly interactive leitmotifs (the referentiality of
which may be either mimetic or conventional) establish emotive, narrative and symbolic articulations of an imaginary, mythic landscape. In a
sense, to use gestaltist terminology, the "evocative" tends to refer to figures, and the "ambient" to grounds. This category (along with its counter-

parts from the "concrete /stylized /ambient" group), also constitutes the staple of science-fiction film soundtracks, suggesting the interest of utilizing new or unfamiliar instruments to evoke unusual or imaginary landscapes. It offers a sonic paradox in the domain of performed music: the *hyperreal* referent of the ambient is precisely an imaginary, *unreal* scene. It is the world fantastically transformed, metamorphosed, derealized. While "notated /stylized /evocative" sounds often refer to the real world, and "notated /stylized /ambient" sounds signify possible worlds, "notated /hyperreal /ambient" ones often indicate improbable, or even impossible, worlds. Consequently, this category suggests a relatively unexplored domain of the sonic poetic imagination.

*

In 1917 — already after the Italian and Russian Futurists and the Dadaists had explored nonsensical syllabic combinations and unexpected microrhythms, so as to decompose language to its poetic least common denominators — Edgar Varèse wrote, in Francis Picabia's journal *391*: "I dream of instruments that will obey thought, and which, with the contribution of a blossoming of unsuspected timbres, lend themselves to whatever combinations I may wish to impose upon them, and yield to the exigencies of my interior rhythm."[109] The initial inspiration came in New York City where Varèse was composing *Amériques* (1918-1921), a work that included, in its vast instrumentation, the curiosities of both a siren and a whip (both of which create glissando effects). Louise Varèse recounts that when Edgar moved into her apartment on 14th Street in Manhattan, "all the river noises entered his room and he discovered the music in the foghorns [....] he listened to the 'parabolas and hyperbolas' of the fire-engine sirens with the haunting music, which he had, thanks to Helmholtz, discovered so long ago. Under the sirens' spell, he transposed their tracings to a number of glissandi..."[110] The sounds of the foghorns, part of "the whole wonderful river symphony," along with the "beautiful parabolas and hyperbolas" of the sirens, revealed a sonic wealth well beyond the tonal limitations of keyboard instruments.

The spell of city noises is a key to sonic modernism, and one might note that other great New York City glissando which appears many years later in a completely different context, Michael Snow's film *Wavelength* (1966-67), a prime example of the role of glissandi in articulating the urban soundscape. While the film unpacks the metaphor of "wavelength" variously as sound waves, light waves, radio waves, sea waves, it also offers a visualization of the glissando:

> *The film is a continuous zoom which takes 45 minutes to go from its widest field to its smallest and final field. It was shot with a fixed camera from one end of an 80 foot loft, shooting the other end, a row of windows and the street. This, the setting, and the action which takes place there are cosmically equivalent. The room (and the zoom) are interrupted by 4 human events including a death. The sound on these occasions is sync sound, music and speech, occurring simultaneously with an electronic sound, a sine wave, which goes from its lowest (50 cycles per second) note to its highest (12000 c.p.s.) in 40 minutes. It is a total glissando while the film is a crescendo and a dispersed spectrum which attempts to utilize the gifts of both prophecy and memory which only film and music have to offer.[III]*

This is certainly one of the longest glissandi in the history of art. It is of interest to ask, as was the case with *Forbidden Planet* a decade earlier, whether or not the soundtrack of *Wavelength* constitutes music. Given the state of musicology of the period — with the acceptance, however marginal, of minimalism, noise, aleatory sources and taped sound as musical possibilities — one can make a strong argument that the glissando in *Wavelength* is indeed musical, or even music.

Varèse's sirens were the prototypes that made Snow's glissando possible. But while Snow staged an electronic glissando wail *as* music, in the 1920s Varèse was still trying to find the proper place of a siren *in* music. Having heard the music in foghorns, he sought the place for foghorns in music. By 1930, believing that the equally tempered chromatic scale had become obsolete, he specified the need for new electric and electronic instruments, to allow the unlimited creation of previously unimagined timbres, enormous increases in energy, and vast spatial complexity. Given the technical limits of the era, he could only approximate the effects he imagined, and these experiments resulted in *Ionisation* (1931), scored for thirteen musicians playing 37 percussion instruments and two sirens (high and low). However visionary this composition might have been, it was only a sketch of his fantasy of an expanded musical spectrum, and it wouldn't be until his introduction to electronic instruments a quarter century later that he would attempt, approximately and belatedly, to instantiate his ideas in the *Poème électronique.*

Early 20th century European music experienced numerous pressures upon the standard system of tonality, well beyond the loosening of the tonal system through extremes of chromatization and experiments in atonality leading to dodecaphony. (The latter shift took place roughly between 1910 and 1920, precisely the years of Italian Futurism and Dadaism.) Foremost among these was a fascination with alternate scales and harmonic systems from folk and foreign musics; complications in rhythm inspired by exotic rhythms and instrumental mechanization (*e.g.*, the player piano, most notably utilized in Conlon Nancarrow's compositions); interest in "non-musical" noises, which motivated an increased use of percussion to enrich and complicate orchestral color; and just intonation. Discussions on noise had for long hinged on Hermann Helmholtz's work on acoustics, with his definition of noise as non-periodic movements of sound waves. Contemporary musicology has not followed this valorization of pure sonic periodicity, because even the most traditional musical instruments produce complex tones due to harmonics, and because a certain amount of "noise" (conceived as sonic irregularity) is necessary for musical enjoyment, since the perfect sonic regularity of pure tones (such as those produced electronically) is aurally less stimulating than tones with complex harmonics.

In a sense, the "noisy" microstructure of musical sound is essential to musical pleasure. In this context, Varèse's choice of percussion and glissandi in *Ionisation* would constitute a watershed in musical composition and theory, by accentuating the use-value of both irregularly pitched and continuous sounds. In doing, so he radically expanded the musical palette, prefiguring the inclusion of "noise," into musical compositions. Percussion had often been described as indefinitely pitched sound, but in fact, there exist no sounds of indefinite pitch, but rather sounds with varied degrees of complex partials, as Jean-Charles François convincingly argues:

> ...one cannot speak of indefinite pitches in themselves, as the treatises suggest, because as we have seen this notion has no real existence, but rather stems from a particular listening attitude. Indeterminate pitches are those that are left as such by the composers themselves, simply because the real pitches of the instruments do not interest them as essential elements of the unfolding of their work.[112]

Varèse's *Ionisation* is emblematic of this situation, insofar as percussion had long been linked to noise (indeterminate pitch), and sirens produce sinusoïdal glissandi that include an infinitude of intermediary pitches in their slide, thus escaping the limitations of the twelve fixed tones of equally tempered scale to which most Western orchestral instruments are tuned, and which most musicians are trained to produce.[113] Reflections upon percussion (an infinite source of irregular tonality, for ultimately any object may become a percussion instrument), electronics (infinite sources of new musical timbres) and glissandi (the infinitude of tonal continuity), radically transformed the limits of music. Music would expand beyond the permutations of a mere twelve tones, with some, like Harry Partch, even arguing for the need to create new instruments, and a new sonic system, for each composition. The musical system henceforth exists not as a function of the organization of the twelve tones of the chromatic scale (whether they be arranged harmonically or serially), but *within* and *between* and *beyond* these notes. In this sense, as Jean-Charles François suggests, "percussion is eminently a subjunctive (of the imperfect tense) in the first person plural."[114] As for the glissando, Francis Bayer, in his study *De Schönberg à Cage*, elaborates:

> *The* glissando *suppresses all possible differentiation between the pitch of sounds; consequently, it establishes a certain relation of incertitude at the heart of sonorous matter, opposed to the somewhat artificial precision of articulated systems: one can even claim that in the* glissando *we are no longer dealing with precise tones, but with a sonorous ensemble movement where, on the spatial plane, only the general direction is really determinable.*[115]

That said, this incertitude does not obviate the potentially mimetic or referential characteristics of such music. Despite the occasional mimesis representing birdsong, automobile horns, anvils, or cowbells in classical music (not to mention the songs of angels and the wails of demons), modernism brought a new theoretical and practical dimension to the role of the anecdotal (if not quite the programmatic) as a mode of referentiality, placing an increasing strain on the supposed abstraction and self-referentiality of the musical system. In a certain sense, as Jean-Charles François stresses, each new instrument (especially exotic ones), "keeps its referential color" as it enters the Western musical domain, with a consequent enrichment of that system.[116] (One must ask in each instance to what degree that referentiality remains. For example, it would seem that as time goes by, the sirens in *Ionisation* are heard less as sirens and more as glissandi.) The notion of *Klangfarbenmelodie* (melody of tone colors) henceforth takes on infinite scope, ultimately leading to *musique concrète*. The "legitimacy" of musical sounds can no longer be judged according to any "musical" scale whatsoever.

By the 1950s, the use of microtones, microharmonies and micropolyphony — whether aleatory or determinate; whether in the form of glissandi, sheets of sound, stochastically oriented sound groups or note clusters — by such composers as Xenakis, Ligeti and Feldman, established a more complex sonorous continuum, structurally homologous to that made possible by electronic sound production. Furthermore, the electronic music of the 1950s and early 1960s is characterized by numerous new sonic possibilities, which can be summed up as follows: the superimposition of sounds through tape mixing; phasing; montage; precise regulation of dynamics; new rhythms; calculation of duration in tape length; rapid speed changes; retrograde forms (reversing tape direction); loops; silence (blank tape); fading (with the resultant change of timbre); fragmentation and distribution of sound (via stereo and multiplex loudspeaker separation). All musical parameters are transformed: pitch, volume, duration, timbre, attack, decay, reverberation, etc. Sine-tone generators allow for pure sounds (without harmonics); white sound generators produce a new sort of noise (simultaneously and equally including all audible frequencies); square-wave generators create new, rich harmonies; filters modify and control complex sound sources; ring modulators combine disparate tones and harmonics; dynamic suppressors eliminate certain sounds and thus control aleatory effects; electronic reverberation simulates and extends the echo effect, variable speed tape recorders transform the concrete.[117] Francis Bayer describes the techniques involved in this expanded use of *Klangfarbenmelodie*: "Perpetual internal transformation of the sonority, always differentiated mixtures of tones, lines and timbres, constant interpenetrations and inmixings of sonorous movements — such are some of the essential characteristics of these types of microstructural organizations for which Ligeti proposed the term 'moving structures.'"[118] These developments not only transformed musical composition, but offered new challenges to musical audition. Ligeti insists that such music need be examined under an "auditory microscope," thus sharpening and transforming the very act of hearing.[119] It is within this expanded musical context that the new role of the glissando must be examined.

*

Iannis Xenakis' electroacoustic piece *La Légende d'Eer* (1977-78) is a musical journey through hell, a decidedly programmatic work variously inspired, as the program notes (a sort of metaphysical listener's guide to the music) indicate, by Plato's myth of Er from *The Republic* (Book X), where a soldier voyages to the land of the dead and returns to tell the tale; Hermes Trismegistos, *Poemandres*; Blaise Pascal, *Pensées;* Jean-Paul Richter, *Siebenkäs*; Robert P. Kirshner, *Supernovas in Other Galaxies*.[120] Not the ancient music of the spheres, but rather the music of an infinitely expanding universe, *La Légende d'Eer* constitutes the musical dimension of Xenakis' multi-media *Diatope* installation, and is of particular importance in the history of the relation between sound and architecture, especially the manner in which sound articulates real and imaginary space, poetic forms and phantasmatic images. In *La Légende d'Eer*, the sound is derived from three musical families: instrumental (African kalimba and Japanese tsouzoumis); noises (*e.g.*, shock of bricks and rubbing of cardboard); mathematically ordered electronic sounds; the work is thus partially concrete, partially performed, partially electronic. (In terms of the present schematization, it thus fall ambiguously into both the "concrete/hyperreal/ambient" and the "notated/hyperreal/ambient" categories.) This musical voyage through hell opens with an almost imperceptible electronic sound: the *étoiles filantes* [shooting stars], as Xenakis refers to them, which, given the varied contexts denoted by the literary sources that inspired the work, can be variously imagined as the sound of instruments, crickets, Morse-like code, or interplanetary signals (akin to the whistlers in Lucier's *Sferics*). This polyvalent complexity suggests that the entirety of the work is programmatically and symbolically overdetermined, and thus need be heard on at least five mimetic levels: natural sounds, musical composition, coded communication, metaphysical allusion, mystical evocation. The opening sounds are musically related to Xenakis' stochastic works such as *Concret PH*, just as the glissandi heard later are related to those of *Metastasis* and *Pithoprakta*, and as the *Diatope* is architecturally related (via the hyperbolic parabolas) to the Philips Pavilion. These initial minimal sounds are both the simulacrum of communication (Morse-like code) indicating that a story is being told, and the evocation of a peaceful natural environment (crickets), a calm soon to be shattered.[121] The piece progressively gains in complexity and intensity, moving from the infinitesimal pianissimo of the simple, soothing opening to an extreme fortissimo coinciding with an increasingly deep layering of the mix, where electronic effects composed in great part of overlapping glissandi build to a horrifying crescendo of hellish, anguish-ridden wails (recalling and far surpassing in terror Henry Cowell's *The Banshee*). Due to the explicit programmatic overdetermination of the work — as well as to the fact that Xenakis was a member of the Greek resistance, and was severely wounded and disfigured during the war — these glissandi are simultaneously to be heard as the threatening hum of over-excited bees, songs of the mythical Sirens, wartime air-raid sirens, the roar of airplanes, whistling shells, explosions, wails of the Harpies, screams of the dying, laments of the dead. One might say that Xenakis stylized and desublimated those very same war sounds earlier valorized and sublimated by Marinetti and Russolo, most notably the Doppler effect of enharmonically changing pitch as shells pass overhead.

In Plato's narrative, Er, a soldier killed in battle, returns from the realm of the dead to tell of both the underworld and of his ascent through the heavenly spheres. Upon each of the eight circles stands a Siren, half-bird, half-woman, singing a single note, whence the harmony of the celestial spheres, and whence the association of the Siren with the afterworld and transcendence. While the Homeric Sirens chant songs of seduction leading to doom, the eight Platonic Sirens sing but one mystical, static, heavenly note apiece. Together, they chant in chorus a chord consisting of all eight notes of the diatonic scale, and they have potentially mastered the sonic material to sing innumerable songs in a variety of modes. In short, the Sirens incarnate music itself. However, with the suppression of the ancient modes in modern harmonized music, and the transformation of the Ionian and Aeolian modes into the major and minor scales, the world had to await several centuries to once again hear the chant of the Sirens.[122]

La Légende d'Eer — after its paradoxically all-too-worldly *and* definitively otherworldly climax, resounding with the wail of the Harpies or the song of the Sirens — gradually winds down in a decrescendo of diminishing intensity and reduction of layers, until the initial *étoiles filantes* return and finally fade away. This repetition of the Morse-like sounds is a sign that the "communications" with which the tale began are coming to an end, this second time experienced as memory traces. The narrator has returned from hell and can now, in a moment of musical circularity, tell the story from the impossible point of view of the dead. The sounds fade into the silence from which they came, and which only the dead may experience.

Yet, it's a long stretch of the imagination from a kalimba and some electronic glissandi to a journey through hell. A detailed analysis of the glissando as a key trope in modernist music will help clarify these matters. For truly, along with the tritone, the glissando is another, perhaps even more potent, *diabolus in musica*. We may elucidate this diabolism with a literary fantasy — inspired by Schönberg's serial dodecaphony and musicologically verified by Adorno — from Thomas Mann's *Doctor Faustus*:

> *We all know that it was the earliest concern, the first conquest of the musician to rid sound of its raw and primitive features, to fix to one single note the singing which in primeval times must have been a howling glissando over several notes, and to win from chaos a musical system. Certainly and of course: ordering and normalizing the notes was the condition and first self-manifestation of what we understand by music. Stuck there, so to speak, a naturalistic atavism, a barbaric rudiment from pre-musical days, is the gliding voice, the glissando, a device to be used with the greatest restraint on profoundly cultural grounds; I have always been inclined to sense in it an anti-cultural, anti-human appeal.*[123]

The glissando constitutes a musical return of the repressed, *i.e.*, the dead, the demonic, the deformed, the unhuman, the monstrous, the impossible.[124] These observations about the disquieting nature of the glissando are supported by contemporary musicological analysis, as in Francis Bayer's analysis:

...in this play of glissandi, clusters *and tone clouds, a sort of will to rediscover a wild, primitive sonorous experience that is always situated beneath or beyond all attempts at systematization. To endow sonorous matter with an articulated and regulatory structure can only be accomplished at the price of a more or less mutilating obliteration of its original sensible qualities and of its truly aesthetic value. It is thus necessary to rediscover, as intact as possible, that primal and immediate musical reality, anterior to all discursive sorts of formations, and to restore all of its expressive powers, generally neutralized and imprisoned by the rules of an artificial organization of cultural origin.*[125]

If the tritone (augmented 4th) was long considered the *diabolus in musica* and prohibited in Medieval times ("mi contra fa diabolus est in musica"), the glissando poses far greater threats to the stability of the harmonic system *and* to the integrity of the melodic line. The tritone, however incommodious, is at least calculable within the theory of harmony. To the contrary, the glissandi, clusters and tone clouds of modernist music — along with the other "noise" fields made possible through percussion and tape — escape determinate calculation and cast music into the realm of the indeterminate (if not, strictly speaking, the aleatory). It would seem that a sort of musical infinitesimal calculus is needed to deal with such effects. The narrator of *Doctor Faustus* continues:

What I have in mind is Leverkühn's preference for the glissando. Of course "preference" is not the right word; I only mean that at least in this work, the Apocalypse, *he makes exceptionally frequent use of it, and certainly these images of terror offer a most tempting and at the same time most legitimate occasion for the employment of that savage device. In the place where the four voices of the altar order the letting loose of the four avenging angels, who mow down rider and steed, Emperor and Pope, and a third of mankind, how terrifying is the effect of the trombone glissandos which here represent the theme! This destructive sliding through the seven positions of the instru-*

ment! The theme represented by howling — what horror! And what acoustic panic results from the repeated drum-glissandos, an effect made possible on the chromatic or machine drum by changing the tuning to various pitches during the drum-roll. The effect is extremely uncanny.[126]

Here Thomas Mann seems to be specifically inspired by Leonardo da Vinci's experiments with friction drums, which Leonardo characterized as an, "appropriate noisemaker for the twelve devils at the gates of hell." Leverkühn's *Apocalypse,* in turn, is a phantasmatic prototype of Xenakis' *Légende d'Eer,* already prefigured in the trombone glissandi of *Metastasis* and *Pithoprakta.* It is not surprising that the potentially open-ended, and thus infinite, extensibility of the glissando (as opposed to the fixedness of singly pitched tones) would have such metaphysical implications, both divine and diabolical. Whence the appropriateness of disquieting pitch changes and extreme glissandi in a work inspired by the biblical Apocalypse.

While acoustically produced glissandi are only potentially infinite (limited by performance technique and instrumental structure), electronic glissandi, as suggested by their use in the quasi-apocalyptic *Légende d'Eer,* are potentially infinite (constrained only by the limits of human audition — and we must not forget that we hear not only with the ear, but with the whole body). These glissandi thus imply, and occasionally invoke, unhuman, inhuman and extrahuman (monstrous) sonic possibilities and imaginary worlds. It is not without interest that Leonardo sought to create an "infinite bow" in the form of a friction wheel or belt. This was apparently one of the inspirations for the particular *intonarumori* that Luigi Russolo — who in *The Art of Noise* (1916) notes the acoustic properties of the whistling of shells — termed the "howler," which emits an uncannily human ululation (related in sound and function to that of the aboriginal Australian bull-roarer). Luciano Chessa, in *Luigi Russolo and the Occult,* notes the relation between this sonic machine and the quest for communications with the dead. The *intonarumori* function as oracular machines, producing, "noises transfigured with a transference of vital energy, recreation of spiritual life which to the living anticipated the beyond and to the dead recalled/ promised life. Not only this: the recreation of spiritual life carried out by the *intonarumori* was the path which conducted the dead toward reincarnation as the final consequence of the materialization of thought forms."[127] Such an orchestra would cause a sonic explosion — a "panic" sense of harmony in nature — whose release of energy would bring cemeteries back to life in a veritable dance macabre.[128] This would permit Russolo to speak of "abstract onomatopoeia," *i.e.*, "the noisy and unconscious expression of the most complex and mysterious motions of our sensibility," a category of sounds of interest in the study of the paradoxical notion of discourse from the point-of-view of the dead: impossible onomatopoeia of impossible worlds. Indeed, the fundamental modernist statement on the glissando, preceded only by Busoni's intuitions about sliding tones, is from Russolo's *The Art of Noise:*

> *All the sounds and noises that are produced in nature, if they are suscepti- ble to variation of pitch (that is, if they are sounds and noises of a certain duration) change pitch* by enharmonic gradations and never by leaps in pitch. *For example, the howling of the wind produces complete scales in rising and falling. These scales are neither diatonic nor chromatic, they are* enharmonic. *Likewise, if we move from natural noises into the infi- nitely richer world of machine noises, we find here also that noises pro- duced by rotary motion are constantly enharmonic in the rising and fall- ing of their pitch.*[129]

These were the considerations that inspired his *intonarumori*, those sonic machines that signalled the beginnings of the polemic concerning the re- lations between noise and musical tones. This resulted in the creation of a new musical symbolism — a sort of sonic transcendence — based on the potentially infinite continuation of the glissando line.

In a different and somewhat more conventional musical context, such otherworldly glissando-based sounds constitute Henry Cowell's miniature composition *The Banshee* (1925), among the first works of Western music totally based on the glissando. These horrifying, ghostly plaints are produced by one musician sweeping the piano strings with both a fingernail and the flesh of the finger to produce glissandi and some pizzicati, while a second musician holds down the damper pedal throughout the performance. Cowell himself suggests the disquieting effects of this little utilized musical device, explaining that the banshee, a spirit of Gaelic folklore, is, "a woman of the Inner World ... who is charged with the duty of taking your soul into the Inner World when you die ... She has to come to the outer plane for this purpose, and she finds the outer plane very uncomfortable and unpleasant, so you will hear her wailing at the time of a death in your family."[130] Through their fleeing pitch and ungraspable line, these glissandi trace the path towards the unknown and unspeakable realm of the underworld. As has no doubt been the case since its origins, music is a process of both evocation and invocation, revealing the wonders of the world and summoning the terrors of the afterworld.

Compare the recent electroacoustic composition by Georgia Spiropoulos, *Klama* (2005-06), for eight part mixed chamber choir of 33 voices with 3 soloists (soprano, contralto and baritone, who at times join the other parts); prerecorded sounds (vinyl records and audio tapes, with their characteristic deterioration of the analogue storage medium and consequent noise); and real time electronics (focusing on distortion, filtering, vocal noise simulation, accentuation of breath, amplitude modulation, granular synthesis) – all combined in hi-fi and low-fi. "The vocal, the electroacoustic and the live electronics parts are interwoven and interdependent; these three levels tend to maximal fusion as if past and present formed a continuous circuit, a new acoustic reality."[131] The three sources of the recorded sonic material are: (a) mourning and speaking voices and ambient noises from an old audio tape recording of a ritual lament *in situ*; (b) excerpts of a Katerina Xirou lament cycle recorded at IRCAM and pressed on vinyl; (c) excerpts of a hymn of the 7th-8th century byzantine funeral mass of Ioannis of Damascus. This work is inspired by Greek *mirolóya* (laments or keening) of the Mani tradition from the south Peloponnesian peninsula. The term *klama* refers to both weeping and ritual lamentations:

> *It characterizes a "polyphony" integrating improvised monodies* (miralóya),
> *epodes, weeping, cries and monologues, accompanied by ritual gestures.*
> *Rather than a chant, the lamentation, by its acoustic violence, may be con-*
> *sidered as an alteration of vocality: an alteration that, due to the emotion-*
> *al shock, equally affects tonality, timbre and language. Practiced by wom-*
> *en, usually in the home before the body of the defunct, this "polyphony" is*
> *a sort of accompaniment and appropriation of the dead, a reorganization*
> *of social structures. This ritual is followed by the byzantine monody of an*
> *orthodox mass celebrated at church. The two forms reunite in a simultane-*
> *ously complementary and opposed manner, in a sort of chaotic acoustic*
> *dissemination and scattering.*[132]

This heart wrenching music — rather than reconciling us with our mortal destiny, as most of the sublime musics of the great religious traditions attempt to do — disturbs, disorients, disquiets. It is a music of anguish and trauma, of fear and trembling unto death. A curious and poignant aside in one of Walter Benjamin's analyses of language is apposite:

> *It is a metaphysical truth that all nature would begin to lament if it were*
> *endowed with language ... Lament, however, is the most undifferentiated,*
> *impotent expression of language; it contains scarcely more than the sen-*
> *suous breath; and even where there is only a rustling of plants, in it there*
> *is always a lament. Because she is mute, nature mourns.*[133]

Such terrible *impotence* makes of lament a form of mourning, and such *un-differentiatedness* calls for its musical elaboration. Writing of the radical "alteration of vocality" inherent in these almost unbearable Mani lamentations, Spiropoulos explains, "the voice is completely deformed, the tonality constantly deviates."[134] This deformation — including voiced gasps, hoarse voices, screams, sobs — is informed by the classic stylizations of ritualized lamentation, and is thus musically coherent, as the composer explains concerning the onomatopeoia in *Klama:*

Women's screams: In Mani, when one says "scream" one often refers to an entire sentence or sometimes a single word that is screamed. As it is impossible to recreate this type of screamed sentence, I opted for fragmentation. The screams one hears in Klama *are either separate words or phonemes extracted from words. Solo baritone and tenors (part B and C): The word* oimoi *(pronounced* imi*) sung by the baritone and taken up again by the tenors roughly means* Alas! *The two* oimoi *come from a short and autonomous melody* (idiomelon) *from the orthodox funeral mass, and it is found several times in Greek tragedy. Tenors (part C): The text is a translation of a popular Mani lamentation:*

> *The earth a tree*
> *Man its fruit*
> *Charon its harvester*
> *Who takes its flower.*[135]

It is hardly surprising that the vocal passages in *Klama* are based, "on single-tone or drone phrases, sometimes including microtonal fluctuations or short glissandi, and continuous ascending glissandi as those observed at the end of phrases/verses of the laments — often, these phrases are to be sung with a continuous raising intensity until exhaled air finishes."[136] The voices of mourners are rent just as the ancients tore their clothes in grief. This musical shock motivates the attempt to express and bemoan death, and it is only appropriate that it would be given over to the human voice, that most complex and subtle of instruments, emanating from our own fragile and mortal viscera. It is once again Thomas Mann who speaks to these issues:

But most shattering of all is the application of the glissando to the human voice, which after all was the first target in organizing the tonic material and ridding song of its primitive howling over several notes: the return, in short, to this primitive stage, as the chorus of the Apocalypse *does it in the form of frightfully shrieking human voices at the opening of the sev-*

enth seal, when the sun became black and the moon became as blood and the ships are overturned.[137]

The effect is metaphysical, theological, aesthetic, psychological, physiological. In terms of structure, "the too simplistic organization of sounds must be placed at the border of pain: a sinusoïdal sound is difficult to tolerate,"[138] and in terms of force, extreme sonic amplitude is painful and destructive, to the point that above a certain decibel level irreparable damage is done to the ears. When one adds hell or the apocalypse as the ultimate referent, such pain becomes absolutely unbearable, and music attains the sublime (or, as the case may be, the counter-sublime), shifting from the mourning for a single person to the breathtaking and terrifying lament for an eternally damned humanity. Such is perhaps the song of the Sirens.

*

The glissando is thus a key trope of modernist music, one that reveals the transcendent, metaphysical, and indeed sublime aspects of the soundscape. However, so as not to leave the impression that the glissando is only a trope of disaster, I would like to conclude this section on a lighthearted note. First, as a comical and dystopian aside (but a historically and musicologically crucial one), the soundtrack to the film *Forbidden Planet* (1956) must be considered as a major precursor to all programmatic electronic music.[139] Composed by Louis and Bebe Barron in their New York studio, the sounds derive from what they termed "organic circuitry" that occasionally self-destructed after one use, producing aleatory and thus unexpected sounds, including many glissandi, the epitome of sci-fi film audio effects. Most of these sounds were produced by ring modulators, with added reverb, delay, reversals and speed changes, all of which were then composed into the component parts of the score. The soundtrack variously evokes the sounds of the extraterrestrial landscape, human and Krell technology, the monster from the Id, and the emotional denotations of the film. A particularly clever moment is the brief demonstration of "Ancient Krell Music," which is stylistically indistinguishable from (or at least bears a striking family resemblance to) the rest of the sound track. This would suggest, within the narrative economy of the film, either that: there is no difference between musical and quotidian sounds in Krell culture (as in John Cage's compositions); or their music derives directly and mimetically from the soundscape of the ambient environment (as is the case for the Kaluli); or the limitations of our human aesthetics do not permit us to distinguish the differences between Krell music and the extraterrestrial soundscapes. Ancient Krell music is thus an allegory of the Barron's music. This musical conundrum is all the more interesting as it implies the elimination of the difference between noise and music, a position heralded by John Cage at the very moment that he was working in the Barron's sound studio in New York in the years just before the film was made. In *Forbidden Planet*, the sound effects are indistinguishable from music, a confusion that accurately illustrates the state of musicology of that period, still unable or unwilling to integrate the tape and electronic revolutions into mainstream musical theory. This joke about the musical equivocation of ancient Krell music took a sadder turn when the film's music won the Academy Award not for best score but for best special effects (indeed, the film credits were not for "music" but rather "electronic tonalities"), and the prize was given not to its creators, the Barrons, but to the special effects team, which had nothing at all to do with the soundtrack. Evidently the members of the Academy of Motion Picture Arts and Sciences also could not distinguish between Krell music and Krell noise.

The second anecdote concerns a Paris concert I attended at the Cité de la Musique that included a performance of John Cage's *4'33"* for chamber orchestra led by a famed conductor who shall remain nameless. At one point during the second movement, a cell phone rang in the pocket of the double-bassist, who answered and proceeded to scold his companion for calling during work hours. This was obviously staged, and not very funny. Furthermore, it meant that the conductor didn't respect the score, which specifically demands performative silence on the part of the musicians. If the phone had rung by accident, it would have been part of the "noise" that constituted the concert (perhaps all the funnier if the phone had been programmed to play the opening notes of Beethoven's *Fifth*, or even one of Cage's compositions). But as a calculated gag, it merely showed disrespect for the score and a lack of understanding of the radical musicological implications of the composition. Cage, who was very sensitive about performances of his work, and who had suffered many such jokes at the hands of uncomprehending and insensitive musicians, would probably have been furious.

The final anecdote is more felicitous, a wonderful moment of musical serendipity and revelation. Several years ago I attended a splendid concert in New York at PS122, of Margaret Leng Tan performing *4'33"* on toy piano. Part way through the second movement of this "silent" piece, the siren of a police car from the precinct around the corner wailed through the streets. According to the score — which indicates that the performer is to remain silent, and that the music consists of all ambient sounds heard during the three movements — the loud, piercing glissando of the siren became part of the performance. This is splendid poetic justice, given Cage's estimation of Varèse and *his* sirens — "rather than dealing with sounds as sounds, he deals with them as Varèse"[140] — as well as the fact that for the New York première of *Ionisation* in March 1933, the two sirens used in the orchestra were lent by the New York City Fire Department.

*

(7) Notated /stylized /evocative. The difference between this category and that of "notated /hyperreal /evocative" is mainly a matter of the degree of stylization. (After all, all representation is in some manner stylization, and this is *a fortiori* the case for music.) For example, if Messiaen's birdsong inspired music for piano falls into the "notated /stylized / evocative" category, his birdsong inspired music for clarinette might rath-

er be part of the "notated /hyperreal /evocative" group, since the timbre and performance capabilities of the clarinette more closely approximate the song of certain birds, with the piano being a greater stylizing factor. The boundaries of all these categories are constantly shifting, and may well be determined as much by changing auditor response as by innate structural features.

Claude Debussy's *La Mer* (1905), one of the greatest works of musical impressionism, is a marvelous evocation of water, composed by the man who insisted: "Listen to the words of no man; listen only to the sounds of the wind and the waves of the sea."[141] Its three movements are highly programmatic: (1) *De l'aube à midi sur la mer. Très lent.* [From dawn to noon on the sea. Very slow.] (2) *Jeux de vagues. Allegro.* [Play of the waves. Allegro.] (3) *Dialogue du vent et de la mer. Animé et tumultueux.* [Dialogue of the wind and the sea. Animated and tumultuous.] I had always wanted to perform the experiment of playing this piece to three different audiences — a random control group of mixed auditors, a class of sound art students, a roomful of sailors — having them all keep weather logs, noting their perception of changing wind speed, wind direction, wave heights, etc. This might sound rather frivolous, but it would offer astonishing listener response information about the very sorts of representational issues of concern here, and would reveal relative degrees of auditor competence concerning specific mimetic factors of music. According to recent studies in statistics, the average of the sum total of the estimates of a group will be closer to the truth than any single guess; *e.g.*, the number of jelly beans in a jar is better estimated by a large group than by a single person. This intuition is certainly related to both stochastics and the "swarm logic" of some animal communities, one which, according to David Toop, may well be relevant to certain aspects of musical group improvisation.[142] This revelation might well open new paths of both sociological investigation in analyzing the perennial desire for utopia, and epistemological or aesthetic studies of imaginary, and even impossible, worlds.

In a similar vein, one may do the following experiment with Kenneth

Anger's beautiful film, *Eaux d'artifice* (1953) — shot in the gardens of the Villa d'Este (Tivoli), famed for its waterworks — with a soundtrack consisting of selections from Antonio Vivaldi's *Four Seasons*. Screen it first with the original soundtrack, then a second time to the accompaniment of Franz Liszt's *Les jeux d'eau à la Villa d'Este*, from his *Années de Pèlerinage* (*Troisième Année;* 1867-1877). Which of the two pieces provides the better musical accompaniment? While Liszt's *Les jeux d'eaux*, as the title suggests, offers a closer aquatic mimesis and a better synchronization with the fountains as filmed by Anger, the Vivaldi effects a broader and more equivocal counterpoint, perhaps more appropriate to the many contrasts and visual contradictions of the film, such as the images of waterworks as fireworks, reaction shots of immobile stone faces, equivocations of scale, contrast of color and b&w, and figuration brought to the point of abstraction. In either case, one might well ask to what degree *Les jeux d'eau à la Villa d'Este* actually represents the waterworks at the Villa d'Este.[140]

To put the question in its most blatant and extreme form, one might also wonder to what extent Ottorino Respighi's *La fontana del Tritone al mattino* or *La fontana di Villa Medici al tramonto*, both from *Fontane di Roma* (1916), could possibly evoke, as the titles indicate, dawn or dusk. Can we really distinguish, by musical cues alone, between the Triton fountain in a Roman piazza and the fountains of the Villa Medici? The diverse sounds of different types of flowing water of the fountains can certainly be imitated, thus we may perhaps be able to musically distinguish between fountains. But can we somehow sonically evoke sunrise or sunset? Appropriate birdsong might have offered a clue, but Respighi seems to have had little concern for ornithology. Clearly, in this regard his representational ambitions are far more modest than those of Messiaen. However, other musical systems do offer precise temporal markers. The extreme codifications of time and season in the Japanese arts, or the precise evocation of emotions keyed to the times of day in Indian ragas, certainly suggest that such mimetic precision is possible, in each case according to the lineaments of a specific symbolic system. The significantly less standardized symbolic codes of

Western cultures usually result in much less evocative musical effects, though there where the programmatic is brought to its utmost degree, as in Wagner, the precision of the leitmotifs reinforces a standardization of codes and thus motivates increased recognition of mimetic effects. In the case of Respighi — unlike Messiaen, where the mimetic reference and the limits of musical representation are pushed to the limit — the precise degree of musical impressionism remains in question. At this point, the problematic is no longer aesthetic and musicological, but psychological and sociological. Here, art enters the realm of fantasy.

*

(8) Notated / stylized / ambient: This category includes almost all Western music, *other than the exceptions that constitute the above seven categories*. Here, referential value is vague, obscure, indiscernible, emotive. In other words, this is the category — consisting of the most familiar sorts of music — where mimesis is most unselfconsciously dissimulated. That said, all the givens of the other categories analyzed above should necessitate a reconsideration of the heretofore extremely limited musicological use-value of mimesis. The hope is that these suggestions will consequently result in the defamiliarization and deconstruction of this most familiar group. To the extent that musical mimesis is increasingly recognized as less marginal and more complex than previously believed, not only will new forms of musical representation most certainly arise, but innovative modes of listening will be demanded for older musical forms. At such a point, the arguments of this essay will have served their purpose, and the schematization of mimetic types will have become obsolete.

CONCLUSION

—

Varieties of Audio Mimesis is a sort of listener's guide, suggesting new ways of hearing novel forms of sound art. In the preceding categories, it is not the precision of categorization that is crucial, but the realization that there exist diverse ontological, epistemological and aesthetic dimensions to all mimesis and representation. Indeed, the very hybridity of modern and post-modern music implies categorical inconsistencies, antinomies, anomalies, so that the schematization necessarily deconstructs in the very process of being written. It is no more than an imperfect tool with a multiple task. Consequently, it is hoped that this brief essay has supported the following theoretical points: (a) *onomatopoeia* is not merely imitation, but also stylization, thus invention; (b) *synaesthesia* guides the metaphoric transfer of sounds, articulating all correspondences according to the inter-relations between the senses; (c) *representation* has become a term of such great equivocation that it is nearly obsolete; however, as the microstructures of mimesis are delineated, its signification becomes precise and its use-value increases; (d) a *symbolic matrix* always contextualizes the structural features of mimesis, which gain meaning from their position within the system; (e) *listening* must be attuned to structurally coherent denotations, as it is all the while further and further lost in the elusive, allusive, illusive domain of connotations, which inexorably leads music to fantasy. It is from these alternate worlds, however familiar or however fantastic, that new musics may arise.

Notes

The dense note mechanism is offered in lieu of a bibliography. A discography seems superfluous given the efficiency of the web. All translations are by the author unless otherwise stated. I would like to thank T. Nikki Cesare, Marcus Gammel, Brandon LaBelle, Christof Migone, Steven Feld, Scott Konzelmann, Helmar Schramm, Georgia Spiropoulos and Gregory Whitehead for their specific comments on the manuscript and their continued sonic inspiration.

1. Henry David Thoreau, *Journal* (1837), Vol. 1 (New York, Houghton Mifflin, 1906), 12.

2. Thoreau, *Journal* (1852), Vol. 3, 219-220. John Cage's fascination with Thoreau — whose modernity is usually underrated — is quite understandable on several levels. Among his many uses of Thoreau's works, consider Cage's lengthy composition/reading *Empty Words*, based on the many quotations from Thoreau's journals dealing with sound. Part 3 of *Empty Words*, recorded live at the Teatro Lirico in Milan, 2 December 1977, was rereleased on Ampersand (ampere 6).

3. *Ibid.*, 349.

4. Leonard Bernstein, *The Unanswered Question* (Cambridge, MA, Harvard University Press, 1976), 424. The *magnum opus* on the chthonic basis of music remains Friedrich Nietzsche, *The Birth of Tragedy* (1872). For a broad assessment of the symbolism of music, see Victor Zuckerkandle, *Sound and Symbol: Music and the External World*, trans. Willard R. Trask (Princeton, Princeton University Press, 1956).

5. Ferruccio Busoni, *Sketch of a New Esthetic of Music* (1911), in *Three Classics in the Aesthetic of Music* (New York, Dover, 1962), 76 and 89.

6. Henry Cowell, *New Musical Resources* (1930; New York, Something Else Press, 1969), 20.

7. See Allen S. Weiss, *Unnatural Horizons: Paradox and Contradiction in Landscape Architecture* (New York, Princeton Architectural Press, 1998), 8-42.

8. James H. Stam, *Inquiries into the Origin of Language* (New York, Harper & Row, 1976), 125.

9.   Roman Jakobson, *Une vie dans le langage* (Paris, Minuit, 1984), 57-58.

10. On the epistemology of correspondences in the arts, see Jonathan Crary, *Techniques of the Observer* (Cambridge, MA, M.I.T., 1992). On universal meanings in phonetics, see Ivan Fónagy, *La vive voix* (Paris, Payot, 1983); and Reuven Tsur, *What Makes Sound Patterns Expressive?* (Durham, Duke University Press, 1992).

11. On the history of differential phonological structures, see *Une vie dans le langage*, 29-61. On the origins of language, Umberto Eco, *The Search for the Perfect Language*, trans. James Fentress (1993; Oxford, Blackwell, 1995).

12. Roman Jakobson, *Six Lectures on Sound and Meaning* (1976; Cambridge, MA, M.I.T. Press, 1978), 113.

13. Claude Lévi-Strauss, "Postscript to Chapters III and IV," in *Structural Anthropology*, trans. Claire Jacobson and Brooke Grundfest Schoepf (1958; New York, Basic Books, 1963), 91. This article is an excellent though brief introduction to the issue of linguistic arbitrariness and motivation from a structural point of view.

14. Ernst Gombrich, *Art and Illusion* (1960; Princeton, Princeton University Press, 1972), 370.

15. M. Grammont, cited in Gérard Genette, *Mimologiques* (Paris, Le Seuil, 1976), 472.

16. *Mimologiques*, 87. For one particularly extreme example, see my analysis of the psychosomatic effects of the glottal occlusive /k/ in the later writings of Antonin Artaud, "From Schizophrenia to Schizophonica," in Allen S. Weiss, *Phantasmic Radio* (Durham, Duke University Press, 1995), 9-34.

17. *Mimologiques*, 399. A classic early study of onomatopoeia is Charles Nodier, *Dictionnaire raisonné des onomatopées françaises* (Paris, Demonville, 1808); see *Mimologiques*, 167-205.

18. On the epistemology of the "prose of the world," see Michel Foucault, *The Order of Things* (1966; New York, Random House, 1970), 17-44; and Maurice Merleau-Ponty, *The Prose of the World*, trans John O'Neill (1969; Evanston, Northwestern University Press, 1973).

19. One would at this point wish to consider how typography inflects meaning; a fine starting point is Johanna Drucker, *The Alphabetic Labyrinth: The Letters in History and Imagination* (London, Thames and Hudson, 1995). One brilliant film of the American avant-garde, Hollis Frampton's *Zorns Lemma* (1970) — a sort

of deconstructed "city film" the core of which is constituted of many series of alphabetically ordered one-second shots of words found in the New York City environment — offers an interesting starting point to investigate the effects of typography on the urban landscape.

20. *Une vie dans le langage*, 31-35; and Peter Steiner, *Russian Formalism: A Meta-poetics* (Ithaca, Cornell University Press, 1984), 140-171 and 199-241. A much-needed study is that of the relations between linguistics and sound art, which will certainly reveal how radical transformations of discursive systems realigned seemingly distant fields. Consider that Saussure's linguistics shared structural homologies with Dadaist poetry (arbitrary disjunction of signifier and signified), Jakobson's studies of linguistic pathologies paralleled Artaud's later writings (corporeally motivated sense of the signifier), and as David Toop argues in *Ocean of Sound: Aether Talk, Ambient Sound and Imaginary Worlds* (London, Serpent's Tail, 1995), 135-136, it was probably no coincidence that, "free improvisation, with the embrace of noise, 'illegitimate' instruments, elements of theater, non-hierarchical organisation and the chance interventions of environmental sounds, coincided with the full emergence of semiotics," especially in the work of Roland Barthes.

21. See *La vive voix*. For some of the more eccentric theories, see the chapter entitled "Myth(étym)ologie" in André Blavier, *Les fous littéraires* (Paris, Veyrier, 1982), 151-230; and Umberto Eco, *Serendipity: Language and Lunacy*, trans. William Weaver (New York, Columbia University Press, 1998).

22. *Mimologiques*, 486-7. These preferences, while relatively marginal in quotidian language, are essential to poetry, most notably where glossographia is used, as in Antonin Artaud's last writings. See Brian Conley and Sina Najafi, eds., "Invented Languages," a dossier and CD in *Cabinet* No. 1 (2000); Jean-Jacques Courtine, ed., "Les glossolalies", *Langages* No. 91 (1988); Brandon LaBelle and Christof Migone, eds., *Writing Aloud: The Sonics of Language* (Los Angeles, Errant Bodies Press, 2001); Jean-Jacques Lecercle, *Philosophy Through the Looking Glass* (La Salle, Open Court, 1985); Michel Pierssens, *The Power of Babel: A Study of Logophilia*, trans. Carl R. Lovitt (1976; London, Routledge and Kegan Paul, 1980); Jed Rasula and Steve McCaffery, eds., *Imagining Language* (Cambridge, MA, M.I.T., 1998); Edward Scheer, ed., *Antonin Artaud* (London, Routledge, 2004); Allen S. Weiss, "Psychopompomania," in *The Aesthetics of Excess* (Albany, State University of New York Press, 1989), 113-134; Allen S.

Weiss, "Libidinous Mannerisms and Profligate Abominations," in *Breathless: Sound Recording, Disembodiment, and the Transformation of Lyrical Nostalgia* (Middletown, Wesleyan, 2002), 115-138.

23. Thoreau, *Journal* (1852), Vol. III, 455.

24. Thoreau, *Journal* (1852), Vol. IV, 328.

25. *Ibid.*, 11.

26. *Ibid.*, 39.

27. Catherine Laroze, *Une histoire sensuelle des jardins* (Paris, Olivier Orban, 1990), 34.

28. Alphonse Karr, *Voyage autour de mon jardin* (1845; Geneva, Slatkine, 1979), 177; cited in *Une histoire sensuelle des jardins*, 44. Synaesthetic experience within the arts is at the core of Romantic aesthetics. For a detailed analysis of this issue, see Julie Ramos, "Un monde de résonances : convergence des arts dans le romantisme allemand," in Serge Lemoine, ed., *Aux origines de l'abstraction* (Paris, Musée d'Orsay, 2003), 198-212.

29. Gaston Bachelard, *L'eau et les rêves : Essai sur l'imagination de la matière* (Paris, José Corti, 1942), 251.

30. Charles Baudelaire, "Du vin et du hachisch, comparés comme moyens de multiplication de l'individualité" (1851), in *Paradis artificiels* (1860), in *Oeuvres complètes*, Vol. 1 (Paris, Gallimard / Pléiade, 1975), 392. On Baudelairian synaesthesia inspired by Wagnerian music, see Allen S. Weiss, "Drunken Space," in *Feast and Folly: Cuisine, Intoxication, and the Poetics of the Sublime* (Albany, State University of New York Press, 2002), 17-37.

31. See the invaluable chronology of the history of synthesized and recorded sound, compiled by Hugh Davies, in Henri Chopin, *Poésie sonore internationale* (Paris, Jean-Michel Place, 1979), 13-40.

32. *L'eau et les rêves*, 48.

33. *Dictionnaire raisonné des onomatopées françaises*, cited in *Mimologiques*, 193-195.

34. Steven Feld, *Sound and Sentiment: Birds, Weeping, Poetics, and Song in Kaluli Expression* (1982; Philadelphia, University of Pennsylvania Press, 1990), 164.

35. *Ibid.*, 168.

36. *L'eau et les rêves*, 261.

37. Steven Connor, *Dumbstruck: A Cultural History of Ventriloquism* (Oxford, Oxford University Press, 2000), 10.

38. Cited in *Mimologiques*, 333.

39. Michel Bras, *Le livre de Michel Bras* (Rodez, Éditions de Rouergue, 1991), 53-77. For the relation between Bras' cuisine, his garden, and the Aubrac landscape, see Allen S. Weiss, *Unnatural Horizons*, 133-137; and "Cuisine et Beaux-Arts : petite méditation sur le gargouillou," *Critique* Nos. 685-686 (2004), a special issue on "La gastronomie" edited by Jean-Claude Bonnet and Allen S. Weiss.

40. *L'eau et les rêves*, 257.

41. *Ibid.*, 253.

42. *Ibid.*, 258.

43. On Japanese poetry and the aesthetics of nature, see Kenneth Yasuda, *The Japanese Haiku* (Rutland, VT, Tuttle, 1957).

44. Cited in *Mimologiques*, 362.

45. Gaston Bachelard, *L'air et les songes : Essai sur l'imagination du mouvement* (Paris, José Corti, 1943), 271. On Mont Ventoux, see Allen S. Weiss, *The Wind and the Source: In the Shadow of Mont Ventoux* (Albany, State University of New York Press, 2005). A fascinating study would be on the representation of wind in music, where each different wind might imply an entire metaphysics. Vladimir Jankélévitch, *La musique et l'ineffable* (Paris, Seuil, 1983), is of great interest in this regard. Consider the following sampling of the names of the winds from Honorin Victoire's erudite and amusing *Petite Encyclopédie des Vents de France* (Paris, Lattès, 2001): L'Al dé Mars, l'Aouro, l'Aurisse, l'Auster folèt, le Balaguère, le Barbanis, le Bén bas, la Bise blanche, la Bise grise, la Bise noire, le Biso, le Bizizel, le Bomwèz, le Bon-Seren, la Borée, la Bourrate, le Calamandrin, le Canigounenc, le Cantalesco, le Carcanet, la Chouillère, le Cirsou, le Cisampo, le Do, le Drailhets, l'Écorche chieuve, l'En-bàs, l'Êt, l'Êti, l'Êtilli, le Foui, la Galerne, le Garbi, le Gargaù, le Grégala, la Hurle...

46. Valère Novarina, *Le Discours aux animaux* (Paris, P.O.L., 1987), 321-328. On the limits of connotation in imaginary ornithological names, see Allen S. Weiss, *Comment cuisiner un phénix* (Paris, Mercure de France, 2004). In *La Chair de l'homme* (Paris, P.O.L., 1995), 509-526, Novarina ends with the actual names of all the rivers of France and Germany, such that the geographic denotation of the rivers is absorbed by the sheer poetry of words and sounds. On Novarina, see Alain Berset, ed., *Valère Novarina : Théâtres du verbe* (Paris, José Corti, 2001).

47. See Roman Jakobson, *Langage enfantin et aphasie* (Paris, Flammarion, 1969).

48. *Inquiries into the Origin of Language*, 205-6.

49. *L'eau et les rêves*, 82.

50. *Ibid.*, 85.

51. *Ibid.*, 259.

52. Thoreau, *Journal* (1852), Vol. III, 457.

53. Olivier Messiaen, *Musique et couleur : Nouveaux entretiens avec Claude Samuel* (Paris, Belfond, 1986), 91. See also Alain Périer, *Messiaen* (Paris, Le Seuil, 1979), 104-129. Such analyses can obviously be transferred to other types of soundscapes, for example in Marcus Gammel and Viktoria Tkaczyk, *L'Europe Folle / Europas Wahn*, a radiophonic work on European shepherd and cowherd calls, broadcast by Deutschlandradio Kultur (Klangkunst) on 30 December 2005 and published on CD as *Europas Wahn. Eine Klangreise in fünf Etappen* (2005).

54. Noted in Don Stap, *Birdsong* (Oxford, Oxford University Press, 2005), 28. This book is an excellent introduction to current research on birdsong. Its pages also contain a vast compendium of birdsong onomatopoeia, of both popular and scientific origin.

55. *Messiaen*, 123.

56. Thoreau, *Journal* (1852), Vol. IV, 31.

57. Pierre Enckell and Pierre Rézeau, *Dictionnaire des onomatopées* (Paris, Presses Universitaires de France, 2003), 49 and 484-5.

58. *Musique et couleur*, 101.

59. *Messiaen*, 125. Messiaen's concern with evoking (if not quite representing) an entire environment is not unlike that of Steven Feld's constitution of the soundscape in *Voices of the Rainforest*.

60. Junichiro Tanizaki, *A Portrait of Shunkin* (1933), in *Seven Japanese Tales*, trans. Howard Hibbett (New York, Vintage, 1996), 51-52.

61. Olivier Messiaen, "Le Merle bleu," liner notes to the CD *Catalogue d'oiseaux*, Books 1-3, Peter Hill, piano (Unicorn-Kanchana, DKP 9062).

62. *L'eau et les rêves*, 253.

63. *Ibid*, 259.

64. Cited in Edward Lippman, *A History of Western Musical Aesthetics* (Lincoln, University of Nebraska Press, 1992), 88. This book contains an excellent survey of the musicological issues related to the aporia between imitation and expression. Perhaps the most extended contemporary consideration of the

tension between the mimetic and the structural aspects of music is T.W. Adorno, *Aesthetic Theory*, trans. C. Lenhardt (London, Routledge & Kegan Paul, 1984). Adorno's musical theory has generated a vast bibliography, beyond the scope of this essay; as a useful overview, see W. Luke Windsor, "Autonomy, Mimesis and Mechanical Reproduction in Contemporary Music," *Contemporary Music Review*, Vol. 15 (1996), 139-150; and Dowing A. Thomas, *Music and the Origins of Language* (Cambridge, Cambridge University Press, 1995).

65. *A History of Western Musical Aesthetics*, 90; 83-136.

66. Philippe Nys, *Le jardin exploré : Une herméneutique du lieu* (Besançon, Éditions de l'Imprimeur, 1999), 128.

67. Paul Ricoeur, *Temps et récit*, Vol. 1 (Paris, Le Seuil, 1983), 76; cited in *Le jardin exploré*, 135.

68. See André Félibien, *Relation de la fête de Versailles du 18 juillet 1668* (1668; Paris, Mercure de France, 1999),

69. On montage as metaphor, see P. Adams Sitney, *Modernist Montage* (New York, Columbia University Press, 1990).

70. See Jean-François Lyotard, *Discours, figure* (Paris, Klincksieck, 1974).

71. Essential is the detailed analysis of classifying systems in Michel Foucault, *The Order of Things*, 125-165, especially 138-145. The origins of such modes of classification are to be found at the beginning of Aristotle's *Poetics*, where he elaborates on the Platonic question of mimesis, describing three modes of imitation according to, "a difference of kind in their means, or by differences in the objects, or in the manner of their imitations." This is, respectively, roughly equivalent to my distinctions between modality, source, and referentiality.

72. I recently presented this schema in an Interart Studies seminar at the Freie Universität of Berlin, directed by Prof. Helmar Schramm, which took place at the Staatlichen Institut für Musikforschung. The presentation met with great resistance, explicitly due to my use of a schema — the participants would obviously have preferred a list, with all of the ensuing paratactic consequences of an open text. I had originally interpreted this as a typical post-structuralist suspicion of the delimiting functions of all categorization. But one philosopher who attended, Anja Brietzke, suggested (perhaps tongue-in-cheek, perhaps not) that the problem was psychologically more profound, and stemmed from the centuries-old influence of Kant's antinomies on the German psyche. Whatever the reason, I take this occasion to again stress that my use of this schema is

for heuristic, and not ontological, purposes. It is provisional and empirical, not essential and metaphysical.

73. David Abram, *The Spell of the Sensuous: Perception and Language in a More-than-Human World* (New York, Pantheon, 1996), 140; see also David Rothenberg, ed., *Music from Nature*, a special issue of *Terra Nova* Vol. 2, No. 3 (1997).

74. Thoreau, *Journal* (1852), Vol. IV, 39.

75. Steven Feld, liner notes to *Voices of the Rainforest* (Rykodisc RCD 10173); for a detailed analysis, see *Sound and Sentiment*. On the theory of soundscape, the *locus classicus* is R. Murray Schafer, *The Tuning of the World* (1977), republished as *The Soundscape: Our Sonic Environment and the Tuning of the World* (Rochester, VT, Destiny Books, 1994).

76. Steven Feld, "Sound as a Symbolic System: The Kaluli Drum," in David Howes, ed., *The Varieties of Sensory Experience* (Toronto, University of Toronto Press, 1990), 89.

77. *Ibid.*, 97.

78. Rick Altman, "The Material Heterogeneity of Recorded Sound," in Rick Altman, ed., *Sound Theory, Sound Practice* (New York, Routledge, 1992), 26.

79. *Ibid.*, 15-31.

80. Steven Feld, email communication with the author.

81. *Birdsong*, 81.

82. See John Harvith and Susan Edwards Harvith, *Edison, Musicians and the Phonograph* (Westport, CT, Greenwood Press, 1987).

83. Steven Feld, "From Schizophonia to Schismogenesis: The Discourses and Practices of World Music and World Beat," in G. Marcus and F. Myers, eds., *The Traffic in Culture* (Los Angeles, University of California Press, 1995), 117. *Voices of the Rainforest* can be heard according to the "day in the life" genre, *i.e.*, a 24 hour investigation of a particular site, such as Walther Ruttmann's classic film, *Berlin, die Symphonie der Grosstadt* (1927), or, in a more musical vein, Messiaen's *Rousserolle Effarvatte* from the *Catalogue d'oiseaux* cycle, which evokes a 24 hour cycle in the life of the bird. Vladimir Jankélévitch's *La musique et les heures* (Paris, Le Seuil, 1988), is a valuable source of inspiration for an extended study of this topic.

84. On sonic ambience, Brian Eno's work is fundamental; see also David Toop, *Ocean of Sound*; and on the intersection of mysticism and spiritualism with modern technologies, Joe Milutis, *Ether: The Nothing that Connects Everything*

(Minneapolis, University of Minnesota Press, 2006).

85. See Iannis Xenakis, *Musique, architecture* (Paris, Casterman, 1976). It is astounding that in Marc Treib, *Space Calculated in Seconds: The Philips Pavilion, Le Corbusier, Edgar Varèse* (Princeton, Princeton University Press, 1996) — which details the extent to which Xenakis was almost totally responsible for the architecture of the pavilion — not only does Xenakis' name not appear in the book's title, but his composition *Concret PH* is mentioned only a few times in passing, while Varèse's *Poème électronique*, discussed in great length, is granted a separate analysis by composer Richard Felciano.

86. See Michael Nyman, *Experimental Music* (New York, Schirmer, 1974), 29-33.

87. See Iannis Xenakis. *Le Diatope* (Paris, Centre Georges Pompidou, 1978).

88. See the special issue of *Film Culture* No. 65-66 (1978), devoted to Paul Sharits.

89. Guillaume Apollinaire, "Le Roi-Lune" (1916), in *Le Poète assassiné* (1916; Paris, Gallimard, 1992), 146-149. Numerous musical, cinematic, and radiophonic works have utilized the same technique; a prime example is Karlheinz Stockhausen's *Telemusik* (1966), an electro-acoustic work composed in Tokyo, but combining sounds from around the globe in the stylistically "symbiotic" manner of what he was to term "global polyphony." See Karlheinz Stockhausen, *Towards a Cosmic Music*, trans. Tim Nevill (Longmead, Element Books, 1989).

90. See Alexandre Scriabine, *Notes et réflexions*, trans. Marina Scriabine (Paris, Klincksieck, 1979).

91. Hollis Frampton, "For a Metahistory of Film," in *Circles of Confusion* (Rochester, Visual Studies Workshop Press, 1983), 111.

92. On the theoretical implications of the heterogeneity of landscape styles, and an analysis of both the *Hypnerotomachia Poliphili* and Les Buttes-Chaumont, see *Unnatural Horizons*, 9-42 and 109-153.

93. See *Internationale situationiste* (Paris, Champ Libre, 1975); and *Robert Smithson: Collected Writings*, ed., Jack Flam (Berkeley, University of California Press, 1996).

94. An extraordinary analysis of the origins of the aleatory in 19th century art is Yves Bonnefoy, "Igitur et le photographe," in Yves Peyré, ed., *Mallarmé 1842-1898 : Un destin d'écriture* (Paris, Gallimard/ Réunion des Musées Nationaux, 1998), 59-85.

95. John Cage interviewed by Daniel Charles, *For the Birds* (Boston, Marion Boy-

ers, 1981), 222; see also Daniel Charles, ed., *John Cage*, a special issue of the *Revue d'Esthétique*, Nos. 13-14-15 (1988); James Pritchett, *The Music of John Cage* (Cambridge, Cambridge University Press, 1993); and of course, John Cage, *Silence* (1961; Cambridge, MA: M.I.T., 1971).

96. Gustaf Sobin, *Luminous Debris: Reflecting on Vestige in Provence and Languedoc* (Berkeley, University of California Press, 1999), 141-142; see also *The Wind and the Source*, 63-74. The classic linguistic study of rhythm in language is Émile Benveniste, "La notion de 'rythme' dans son expression linguistique," in *Problèmes de linguistique générale*, Vol. 1 (1951; Paris, Gallimard, 1966), 327-335.

97. Scott Konzelmann, email of 22 September 2005.

98. While Cage is most often credited with transforming noise into music, it should not be forgotten that his compositions also occasionally transform music into noise, as in his *Opera Mix*, or his proposal to perform all of Beethoven's symphonies simultaneously. For a very different perspective, sociological and political rather than aesthetic, see Jacques Attali, *Noise: The Political Economy of Music*, trans. Brain Massumi (1977; Minneapolis, University of Minnesota Press, 1985).

99. Pauline Oliveros, cited in *Ocean of Sound*, 248-249. Such extreme echo and reverb effects are related to issues in theater design, which has taken enormous strides with the advent of computer simulated concert hall acoustics, such as those of the New York firm Artec Consultants Inc. These simulations reveal acoustic changes in virtual spaces modelled on actual concert halls, such that the sonic effects of architectural and design transformations can be determined in advance. In a sense, these programs are super-complex echo and reverb producing machines. On theatrical acoustics and the spatiality of sound, see Brandon LaBelle and Steve Roden, eds., *Site of Sound: of Architecture & the Ear* (Los Angeles, Errant Bodies Press, 1999); Robert E. Apfel, *Deaf Architects & Blind Acousticians: A Guide to the Principles of Sound Design.* (New Haven, Apple Enterprises Press, 1998); and for the pre-digital era, George C. Izenour, *Theater Design* (New York, McGraw-Hill, 1977). For a fascinating sonic investigation of unusual sites, see the book and accompanying CD by Louise K. Wilson, *A Record of Fear* (Cambridge, National Trust and Commissions East, 2006), a documentation of sonic art works created in the now-abandoned top-secret military testing grounds of Orford Ness in Britain.

100. Gregory Whitehead, email of 19 July 2006. Whitehead's engagement with noise

is epitomized by his series of "screamscapes" of different cities, beginning with that of Sydney, documented in the radiophonic work, *Pressures of the Unspeakable* (1989); see *Phantasmic Radio*, 75-92.

101. One of the best compendiums of such serendipitous sonic events is David Toop, *Ocean of Sound*; one stunning example is the discovery of dub by Osbourne Ruddock (King Tubby) in the late 1960s.

102. The article in question is Allen S. Weiss, "Between the Sign of the Scorpion and the Sign of the Cross" (1986), in *The Aesthetics of Excess*, 163-180.

103. Tony Conrad, "LYssophobia: On FOUR VIOLINS," liner notes to *Early Minimalism* (Table of the Elements AS33), 23-24. Perhaps the most extreme example of the minimal and purified musical investigation of the glissando is Tony Conrad's *Fantastic Glissando* (1969), as always with his work, on the border between experimentation, performance and composition.

104. Yasunari Kawabata, *Snow Country* (1956), trans. Edward G. Seidensticker (New York, Berkeley Medallion Books, 1960), 127.

105. Kakuzo Okakura, *The Book of Tea* (1906; New York, Dover, 1964), 35. The great specialist of Zen Buddhism, Daisetz T. Suzuki, also described the sounds in a tea ceremony: "The breeze passing through the needles of the old pine tree harmoniously blends with the sizzling of the iron kettle over the fire," in *Zen and Japanese Culture* (New York, MJF Books, 1959), 274. Here the choice of onomatopoeia is unfortunate, for while the kettle might well have been *sizzling*, it is hardly this sound that would harmonize with the wind.

106. Kyn Taniya, "IU IIIUUU IU," in *Radio: Poema inalámbrico en trece mensajes* (1924); see Rubén Gallo, *Mexican Modernity: The Avant-Garde and the Technological Revolution* (Cambridge, MA, M.I.T. Press, 2005), 117-167.

107. John Cage, "The Future of Music: Credo" (1937), in *Silence*, 4.

108. See Richard Toop, *György Ligeti* (London, Phaidon, 1999), 120-121. Ligeti made extensive use of glissandi in his compositions, and one of his early pieces was entitled *Glissandi, elektronische Komposition* (1957).

109. Cited in Odile Vivier, *Varèse* (Paris, Le Seuil/Solfèges, 1973), 91; see also Francis Bayer, *De Schönberg à Cage : Essai sur la notion d'espace sonore dans la musique contemporaine* (Paris, Klincksieck, 1987), 130-33. Among the many works that reconsider the various paradigm shifts in modernist music, note: Paul Griffiths, *Modern Music: The Avant-Garde Since 1945* (New York, Braziller, 1981); Michael Nyman, *Experimental Music* (New York, Schirmer, 1974); Douglas

Kahn and Gregory Whitehead, eds. *Wireless Imagination: Sound, Radio, and the Avant-Garde* (Cambridge, MA, M.I.T. Press, 1992); Jean-Pierre Criqui, ed., *Synesthésies/Fusion des Arts*, a special issue of *Les Cahiers du Musée national d'art moderne*, No. 74 (2000-2001); Danièle Cohn, ed., *Musique(s) : Pour une généalogie du contemporaine*, a special issue of *Critique*, No. 639-640 (2000); Brandon LaBelle, *Background Noise: Perspectives on Sound Art* (New York / London, Continuum, 2006).

110. Louise Varèse, *Varèse: A Looking Glass Diary* (New York, Norton, 1972), 101.

111. Michael Snow, cited in *Film-Makers' Cooperative Catalogue* No. 6 (New York, Film-Makers' Cooperative, 1975), 232. In fact, Snow's description of his own glissando is faulty, since near the end of the film, multiple ascending and descending glissandi are mixed with the major ascending line. In consideration of the musicality of the soundtrack to *Wavelength*, the fact that Snow is an accomplished free-jazz pianist is not without interest. In more general terms, a revisionist reading of the history of avant-garde film from the point of view of the various sound arts is needed to reveal the interactions, inspirations, exchanges and derivations at work in the exceedingly complex and interactive New York City art scene of the 1960s. One should not be too surprised to discover that filmmakers and musicians in the same time and place were doing similar things to tape, such as micromontage, phasing, the use of blank tape and noise, slow and fast motion, tape reversal, extreme dynamics, etc.

112. Jean-Charles François, *Percussion et musique contemporaine* (Paris, Klincksieck, 1991), 95; see his brilliant analysis of *Ionisation*, 109-139.

113. On the role of the glissando in modernist sound art, see the section on "The Gloss of the Gliss," in Douglas Kahn, *Noise, Water, Meat* (Cambridge, MA, M.I.T. Press, 1999), 83-91.

114. *Percussion et musique contemporaine*, 283; see Daniel Charles, *Musiques nomades* (Paris, Éditions Kimé, 1998); and Allen S. Weiss, "Le désoeuvrement de la musique," *Critique* No. 639-640 (2000).

115. *De Schönberg à Cage*, 124.

116. *Percussion et musique contemporaine*, 40. Others, like Boulez, saw such referential or anecdotal incursions as a sort of contamination; see Pierre Boulez, *Penser la musique aujourd'hui* (Paris, Denoël/Gonthier, 1963), 19. For a brilliant reconsideration of the relations between the visual and the sonic, a groundbreaking work is the catalogue of the Musée d'Orsay exhibition, Serge Lemoine and Pascal

Rousseau, eds., *Aux origines de l'abstraction : 1800-1914* (Paris, Réunion des musées nationaux, 2003), especially Marcella Lista, "Le rêve de Prométhée : art total et environnements synesthésiques aux origines de l'abstraction," 214-229, and Pascal Rousseau, "'Arabesques': le formalisme musicale dans les débuts de l'abstraction," 230-245. This exhibition proposed a sort of unified field theory of aesthetics organized by the belief in the convergence of wave theories (sonic and visual) within synaesthetic sensibility, such that the visual morphology of sound waves (color harmonies and arabesque rhythms) was linked to the origins of abstract painting. This catalogue should be read alongside the earlier catalogue of the exhibition *The Spiritual in Art: Abstract painting 1890-1985*, edited by Maurice Tuchman with Judi Freeman (Los Angeles and New York, Los Angeles County Museum of Art/Abbeville Press, 1986). While the Orsay volume stresses the scientific origins of abstraction, the LACMA project focuses on the spiritual, and more particularly the theosophic, influences. Both exhibitions would support considerations of the extreme limits of audio mimesis, the Orsay show on the perceptual dimension, the LACMA show on the transcendental dimension.

117. This list is compiled from H. H. Stuckenschmidt, *Twentieth Century Music* (New York, McGraw-Hill, 1969), 174-192. While in certain ways this book is outdated, the chapter dealing with electronic music, "Technical sound-material," is particularly useful in the present context, insofar as it was written from the perspective of pre-digital musical synthesis, and thus gives a good sense of the possibilities and limits of electronic musical works of that period.

118. *De Schönberg à Cage*, 139.

119. *Ibid.*, 137. Notable in this context is one of Cage's earliest compositions, *Imaginary Landscape No. 1* (1939), a work utilizing one microphone picking up percussion sounds (derived from a Chinese cymbal and a piano played both by brushing the bass strings and muting the strings by hand while playing the keys) and a second microphone used to pick up acoustic test recordings (*i.e.*, electronic sounds, mainly glissandi) played on a turntable (the notation indicates rhythm by determining speed changes on the turntable and lifting the needle on and off the disks.) This groundbreaking work already hinted at live electronic music, DJ mixing, extended notions of rhythm, prepared piano, radical microphony, concrete music. The origins and early history of *musique concrète* are contained on the CD *Pierre Schaeffer : L'oeuvre musicale* (INA.GRM /

Librairie Séguier: INA C 1006-1007-1008-1009); one should also consult Pierre Schaeffer, *Traité des objets musicaux* (Paris, Le Seuil, 1966). For some of the contemporary implications of this tradition, especially in terms of the radical use of the microphone, see Christof Migone, *Sound Voice Perform* (Los Angeles, Errant Bodies Press, 2005); and Paul D. Miller, *Rhythm Science* (Cambridge, MA, M.I.T. Press, 2004). On the question of the transformation of hearing, Peter Szendy, *Écoute : Une histoire de nos oreilles* (Paris, Minuit, 2001).

120. One might wish to compare the radiophonic work by Andreas Ammer, *Radio Inferno* (Hörspiel Bayerischer Rundfunk, 1993), a contemporary multi-lingual version of Dante's masterpiece. Some other hellish auditory voyages would include Krzysztof Penderecki, *Threnody for the Victims of Hiroshima* (1959-61); Luciano Berio, *Visage* (1961); Luigi Nono, *Ricorda cosa ti hanno fatto in Auschwitz* (1965); Sylvano Bussotti, *La passion selon Sade* (1979); György Ligeti, *Le Grand macabre* (1974-77). As an aside, it should be noted that the annals of Art Brut contain numerous examples of extraterrestrial and afterworldly communications; particularly compelling is Jeanne Tripier, whose works have often been examined, for example in Allen S. Weiss, "Psychopompomania," in *The Aesthetics of Excess*, 112-134.

121. Thoreau, as might be expected, attempted cricket onomatopoeia, rendered as *creaking* or *shrilling* in the 27 July 1852 entry of his *Journal* Vol. IV, 264; the noun *cricket* nevertheless provides its own best onomatopoeia. Compare the beginning of *La Légende d'Eer* with John Hudak's *Pond* (1998; privately pressed CD), a work of extreme minimalism, delicate rather than severe, inspired by Japanese aesthetics, evoking the sounds of evening crickets at an isolated pond. Both the CD and the jewel box covers are simply white, with no other indications than "john hudak, pond" printed in tiny letters as a sort of Zen exercise in design. This is simultaneously a work of ecological evocation and the far-reaching electronic investigation of a small group of small sounds. This bears further comparison with works written for the Japanese shakuhachi flute, always attuned, like haiku poetry, to the natural environment; to cite one example: *Matsukaze* (Wind Through Pine Trees), as performed by Yoshikazu Iwamoto (Qualiton: Musique du Monde CD, 92543-2). The play of correspondences in Japanese music is profound: Lucas Foss once characterized Toru Takemitsu's music as a form of landscape painting. In both East and West, the question of evocation is ancient. Consider, for example, Leonardo da Vinci's claim that

gazing into fire, old walls, or the marks left by a sponge soaked in ink and thrown against a wall will reveal the most complex and strange landscapes and battles. This serendipity also has a sonic version, as Leonardo explains that, "in such walls the same thing happens as in the sound of bells, in whose stroke you may find every named word which you can imagine." Cited in E.H. Gombrich, *Art and Illusion: A Study in the Psychology of Pictorial Representation* (Princeton, Princeton University Press, 1960), 188.

A contemporary musical work that offers numerous structural and audiophonic homologies to *La Légende d'Eer* is Pierre Henry's *Cortical Art III* (1973, Phillips). This work consists of a solo improvisation on Roger Lafosse's Cortical Art synthesizer, which transforms brainwaves into sounds. The opening sounds like avant-garde acoustic organ music, soon transformed into electric organ music, afterwards evolving into electronic music, and finally building to a crescendo of noise music. There are moments that resemble the crescendo of *La Légende d'Eer*, and others that evoke parts of *Forbidden Planet*, especially the sonic evocation of the Monster from the Id. It is tempting to imagine that since Henry's piece is generated by brainwaves, certain moments may indeed be literally derived from the libido. I would like to thank Jared Ellison for bringing this work to my attention, through the brilliant analysis he wrote for my course on "Sound and Image in Experimental Cinema" at NYU (2007).

122. On the song of the Sirens, both seductive and terrifying, see Pascal Quignard, *La haine de la musique* (Paris, Calmann-Lévy, 1996), 179-200. In terms of historical precedents, around 1903 the Dutch mathematician Henri A. Naber apparently conceived of an orchestra of sirens, a project currently under study by John Heijmans.

123. Thomas Mann, *Doctor Faustus* (1947), trans. H.T. Lowe-Porter (New York, Vintage, 1992), 374.

124. On the musical potentials of these extreme sonic possibilities, see David Toop, *Haunted Weather: Music, Silence and Memory* (London, Serpent's Tail, 2004).

125. *De Schönberg à Cage*, 129-30. Bayer's analysis seems to be a direct gloss on Mann's fantasies. In a very different context, it was pointed out to me by musician and musicologist Michael Gallope that part of the scandal around the early singing of Bob Dylan was a result of his vocal distentions — glissandi, in effect — that bent and stretched the voice in what was then an unacceptable manner in the folk music tradition.

126. *Doctor Faustus*, 374-75

127. Luciano Chessa, *Luigi Russolo and the Occult* (Ann Arbor, UMI, 2004), 260. Chessa notes that Maurice Ravel heard Russolo's intonarumori in 1921, and was inspired to use it for the glissando passages of *L'Enfant et les sortilèges*, though they were finally scored for more conventional instruments.

128. *Ibid.*, 244.

129. Luigi Russolo, *The Art of Noise*, trans. Barclay Brown (1916; New York, Pendragon Press, 1986), 63.

130. Henry Cowell, cited in Mark Evan Bonds, *A History of Music in Western Culture* (Upper Saddle River, Pearson/Prentice Hall, 2006), 441. Strictly speaking, *The Banshee* should be placed in the "notated/hyperreal/evocative" section, since it is a creature (however imaginary) rather than an ambience that is invoked. An interesting bit of trivia is that the 29 August 1952 concert at the Maverick Concert Hall in Woodstock, New York, that premiered Cage's *4'33"* also presented *The Banshee*. This is all the more interesting as Cowell was one of Cage's teachers, and Cowell's invention of directly manipulating piano strings was a source for Cage's prepared pianos.

131. Georgia Spiropoulos, "KLAMA: The Voice from Oral Tradition in Death Rituals to a Work for Choir & Live Electronics ," published in the proceedings of the 4th Sound and Music Computing Conference (11-13 July 2007, Lefkada, Greece). As *Klama* remains unpublished and unreleased to date, I offer a somewhat lengthy description of the piece.

132. Georgia Spiropoulos, program notes to the premiere performance of *Klama* (10 June 2006), part of the Théâtre de la Voix concert, Festival Agora, Centre Georges Pompidou, Paris. Spiropoulos's work is deeply influenced by her compatriot Xenakis, in terms of her acuity regarding the possibilities of new technologies and her attentiveness to extra-musical signification, though it differs in her profound concern with issues of feminine expression. Note that the French *cri* can be translated as scream or cry.

133. Walter Benjamin, "On Language as Such and on the Language of Man" in *Reflections*, trans. Edmund Jephcott (New York, Harcourt, Brace, Jovanovich, 1978), 329.

134. Georgia Spiropoulos, email of 29 December 2005. Compare Xenakis' *Kassandra* (1987), especially as interpreted by the extraordinary baritone Spiros Sakkas. Given the *a fortiori* desublimatory nature of the glissando, it is appropriate that

Annette Michelson concludes her study of glossolalia, scatological desublimation and abstraction by claiming (in one of the most subtle euphemisms for flatulence that I have yet encountered): "the poetics of anal glossolalia may be seen as the hyperbolic instance of the sliding of signifier over signified in the choreographic movement of a glissade," in Annette Michelson, "De Stijl, Its Other Face: Abstraction and Cacaphony, or What Was the Matter with Hegel?" *October* No. 22 (1982), 25; see the chapter on "Flatus Vocis: Somatic Winds" in Christof Migone, *Sonic Somatic: Performances of the Sonic Body* (doctoral thesis, Department of Performance Studies, New York University, 2007), 106-134.

135. Georgia Spiropoulos, email of 25 August 2006.

136. Cited in "KLAMA: The Voice from Oral Tradition in Death Rituals to a Work for Choir & Live Electronics."

137. *Doctor Faustus* 375. It is not surprising that Ligeti cites *Doctor Faustus* as a major influence on his opera, *Le Grand Macabre.*

138. *Percussion et musique contemporaine,* 31. Pain and hearing loss is a function of the amplitude and duration of a noise; according to the National Institute of Health, it is generally agreed that extended exposure to over 85 decibels should be avoided, prolonged exposure to over 90 decibels can cause gradual hearing loss, and exposure to 110 decibels for over one minute risks permanent hearing loss.

139. The originality of both *La Légende d'Eer* and the soundtrack to *Forbidden Planet* should be placed in the perspective of the early history of electronic music, which is beyond the scope of this essay. As an introduction, I recommend the excellent CD anthology *Pioneers of Electronic Music* (CRI CD 611). On the subject of *Forbidden Planet,* I would like to register a protest. Given Michel Chion's always astute, and often brilliant, analyses of sound in cinema (*La voix au cinéma* and *Le son au cinéma*), his shortsighted estimation of the soundtrack of *Forbidden Planet,* as "primitive" in relation to contemporary electronic music of the same epoch, comes as a surprise: "That warm rain of electronic sounds, continuously washing down the soundtrack of a galactic tale, well corresponds to the most widespread cliché of electroacoustic music: that it only exists to illustrate spaceships and little green men," in *La musique électroacoustique* (Paris, Presses Universitaires de France, 1982), 77. First of all, this soundtrack isn't a cliché, but a paradigm, given its historic precedence. Furthermore, Chion's recourse to metaphors that are themselves clichés, rather than a more formal

musicological analysis, suggests a certain disingenuousness, and he would have done well to consider all that is revolutionary in this soundtrack: the aleatory nature of the "organic circuitry," the importance of the glissando, the symbolism of Krell aesthetics, etc. It is also quite disappointing that, rather than investigating the role of audio mimesis in its age-old musicological context, he simply disparages the illustrative aspect of this music. He might have had a very different experience of the piece had he listened to the CD rather than just viewing the movie, as this degree of abstraction accentuates the musicality of the soundtrack.

140. John Cage, "Edgard Varèse" (1958), in *Silence*, 84.

141. Cited in *Ocean of Sound*, 173.

142. *Haunted Weather*, 30-32.

143. A beautiful exploration of the metaphor of film and the river flowing is Paul Sharits, *S:TREAM:S:S:ECTION:S:ECTION:S:S:ECTIONED* (1968-71); see *Film Culture* Nos. 65-66 (1978); on water sounds in modernist music, see the section "Water Flows and Flux" in *Noise, Water, Meat*, 242-288.

Varieties of Audio Mimesis: Musical Evocations of Landscape
ISBN 978-0-9772594-4-1

Errant Bodies Press, Berlin/Los Angeles
Audio Issues Vol. 3
www.errantbodies.org
Copyright 2008
Second printing 2011

Design: fliegende Teilchen, Berlin
Printed: Druckerei Conrad, Berlin

Inserts: Hieronymus Bosch (c.1450–1516), "The Concert in the Egg
(satire of alchemy symbolized by a philosophical egg)," Palais des Beaux Arts,
Lille, France. Photo: Réunion des Musées Nationaux/Art Resource, New York

David Teniers, "Katzenkonzert," 1635, Bayerische Staatsgemäldesammlungen,
Alte Pinakothek Munich. Photo©: Joachim Blauel – ARTOTHEK

Errant Bodies publications are distributed by DAP, New York
www.artbook.com